THE MÄSTERMYR FIND

THE MÄSTERMYR FIND

A Viking Age Tool Chest from Gotland

By

Greta Arwidsson and Gösta Berg

SkipJack Press
In cooperation with Larson Publishing Company

5995 149th Street West, Suite 105,
Apple Valley, MN 55124

Publisher's Cataloging-in-Publication
(*Provided by Quality Books, Inc.*)

Arwidsson, Greta, 1906-
    The Mästermyr find   a Viking age tool chest
from Gotland / by Greta Arwidsson and Gösta Berg.
    p. cm.
    Includes bibliographical references and index.
    Originally published in 1983 by Kungl. Vitterhets
Historie och Antikvitets Akademien, Stockholm, Sweden
    ISBN· 0-9650755-1-6

    1. Gotland (Sweden)--Antiquities. 2. Northmen
--Sweden--Gotland. 3. Archaeology Medieval.
4. Tools--Sweden--Gotland. 5. Vikings.   I. Berg,
Gösta, 1903- II. Title.

DL971.G7A78 2000   948.6
                QBI99-1859

Published by arrangement with and permission of
Kungl. Vitterhets Historie och Antikvitets Akademien
(The Royal Academy of Letters, History and Antiquities)
Stockholm, Sweden

Printed in the United States of America

ISBN   0-9650755-1-6

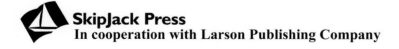

SkipJack Press
    In cooperation with Larson Publishing Company

5995 149th Street West, Suite 105,
Apple Valley, MN 55124

www.finneyco.com • www.astragalpress.com

Contents

Contents

Preface

The publication of this work has been considerably and regrettably delayed. At the end of the 1940s the late Professor Mårten Stenberger then curator at the State Historical Museum in Stockholm, suggested that he and one of the present authors Gösta Berg, should together publish a monograph of the great find discovered in 1936 in Mästermyr on Gotland. Stenberger was to have been responsible for the archaeological aspects of the find, and Berg for the ethnological aspects. The work began in earnest in 1952 when the artist Janis Cirulis (chief designer at the Opera in Riga before the war and now living in the USA) was commissioned to draw all the objects in the find. Cirulis, who had previously been employed at the Nordiska Museet, carried out the work in close collaboration with Stenberger and the resulting drawings deserve the highest praise. The find was photographed with great skill by Märta Claréus later chief photographer at the Nordiska Museet. On Berg's suggestion the wood was analysed by the late Professor Torsten Lagerberg and some metallographic studies were arranged by the late Professor Erik Rudberg, then head of the Metallographic Institute. The results of these studies are given here as appendices Another appendix is a study of some geological and plant-geographical conditions at Mästermyr carried out at our request by the late Professor Gösta Lundqvist, then State Geologist. In the same year Berg and Stenberger travelled to Norway on a grant from *Humanistiska fonden* to study comparative material in the collections.

Stenberger became Professor at the University of Uppsala in 1952, and a few years later Berg became head of the Nordiska Museet and Skansen. There was a great deal of new work to be done and the Mästermyr material was left to one side. Before his death on January 19th 1973 Stenberger had advanced plans to resume the work and had obtained a grant from *Statens Humanistiska forskningsråd* for travel on the Continent to study comparative material. He planned a broader study of relevant problems based on the Swedish find.

On Stenberger's death, his place in the project was taken by Professor Greta Arwidsson. The two authors Arwidsson and Berg, are now jointly responsible for the present publication. The scope of this study is not the same as that envisaged by Stenberger Since many general surveys of tools and iron manufacturing techniques have now been published, we have felt justified in restricting the discussion of comparative material. The detailed description of the find through text and illustration, and a discussion of its date, are therefore accompanied by only short references to the development and distribution of these tool types before the medieval period and to how they might have been used, on the basis of a comparison with tools of a later date and a consideration of ethnological archival material.

Although there has been consultation between the authors, each author is responsible for his or her own sections. Greta Arwidsson compiled the catalogue, having also been responsible for the preliminary cataloguing of the find while employed at the State Historical Museum in 1937

Stefan Krig helped with checking some of the archival material and illustrative material. Elisabeth Aiken-Almgren assisted Greta Arwidsson, particularly with the layout of the illustrations. The excellent translation work has been performed by Eva Wilson and Simon Wilson, London.

Editing and layout by Greta Arwidsson.

We gratefully acknowledge the receipt of grants from the Swedish Council for Research in the Humanities and the Social Sciences and from Berit Wallenberg Foundation as well as the support of Nordiska Museet and Statens Historiska Museer Stockholm.

Stockholm, March 1982

Greta Arwidsson   *Gösta Berg*

1. The circumstances of the find
by Greta Arwidsson

The chest, tools and other material were found during ploughing in the field Mästermyr 1[8] in October 1936. The field is in Snoder Sproge, and was owned by Emil Norrby The finder was Hugo Kraft, a farmer from Rone, formerly of Hemse.

The find was preserved in its entirety through the intervention of Karl Jacobsson of Ringome, Alva, an artisan with an interest in local history and the representative of the Central Board of National Antiquities for the Hemse area from 1928 to 1942.

Jacobsson s report to the Central Board of National Antiquities is the earliest account of the circumstances of the find. Some further details are derived from contemporary notices in the local press and from information given by the landowner to Mårten Stenberger a year later Further interesting details were related to Greta Arwidsson in 1979 by the finder Hugo Kraft, and his wife Maria (see below)

Jacobsson s letter to the Central Board of National Antiquities, dated October 30th 1936, contained the following information:

While working in a field in Sproge, Hugo Kraft, a farmer from Hemse, uncovered in the so-called Mästermyr at a depth of $\frac{1}{2}$ *aln* (c. 30 cm) a copper cauldron, an oak chest containing all manner of iron goods, chains, axes, sledge-hammers, hammers, saws, and also including a steelyard of fine workmanship, I believe gold-plated, several keys, art-work, a smith's tongs, several boring-bits etc. etc. Everything together weighing at least 40 kg.

The newspaper *Gotlands Allehanda* published the first article on the find on November 6th 1936. It describes how the ploughshare first brought up a copper cauldron and then, returning to the same place along the next furrow stuck fast again, this time on an old oak chest. On November 10th the same paper adds one more item of information: the chest had a fairly thick chain 'wrapped round it'

On the instruction of the State Antiquary Erik Bohrn (Inspector of Ancient Monuments) examined the site early in November 1936. At that time pieces of rust and rust traces could still be seen on the surface of the field, but as the ground was waterlogged a closer examination could not be made. No fragments of iron or organic material, which could have been associated with the find, were collected on this occasion nor was the site marked or its position fixed. Bohrn then collected the find from Jacobsson, who had apparently picked up most of the objects from the site of the find before sending his report to the State Antiquary

Not until the following autumn did the then Inspector of Ancient Monuments for Gotland Mårten Stenberger attempt an investigation. As the site was not marked he decided to open trial trenches over an area of about 375 square metres.

The following is a summary of Stenberger's report to the State Antiquary dated September 28th 1937

The site of the find is a field in Mästermyr recently brought under cultivation. According to the maps in the Land-Survey Office of Gotland *län* the field occupies the eastern part of the plot Sproge Mästermyr 1[8] The reclaimed land borders on Eske träsk, the swamp which existed here before the draining of Mästermyr The probable site of the discovery of the chest, based on the sketch survey made during my investigation, is marked on this map by a circle (cf. map. Pl. 31). It can be seen that the chest was discovered quite close to the border with Silte parish, just at the eastern edge of Eske träsk, between this former swamp and the larger Risala träsk. Plot 1[8] projects southwards within the area of Silte parish, which surrounds it on three sides (see Pl. 31). As stated in earlier reports, the owner of the field is Emil Norrby a farmer from Snoder Sproge.[1]

Stenberger's trial trenches were about 75 cm wide and 50 cm deep.

The soil consisted of a layer of peat 20–25 cm thick resting on lake marl. The limestone bedrock lay about 50 cm below the surface of the marl. Throughout the whole area the lake marl below the peat appeared to be undisturbed and no objects, rust traces or anything else of note were observed during excavation. The oak chest and the objects lying beside it had probably sunk some way into the lake marl. (Stenberger's description in a report in ATA.)

Stenberger suspected that the site which had been pointed out to him was incorrect. Considering the size of these open fields it is not surprising that after a time a

---

Sture Norrby emphasises that the site of the find is in Sproge parish and not, as often stated, in Silte parish. He also points out that his father Emil Norrby is wrongly described as the finder in Press, 1974, p. 328.

mistake might be made if the site had not been marked or plotted on a map.

Greta Arwidsson visited the site in July 1979 with Sture Norrby the present owner of Snoder In the autumn of the same year after the potato harvest, she investigated an area of about 2000 square metres with Sven Östman (Kvie, Stenkyrka) metal detector expert of the Central Board of National Antiquities Gotland division. At the same time ten trial pits were excavated down to the sterile lake marl.

The metal detector reacted to a variety of small iron objects and fragments in the field, but these were all obviously of recent origin. The results of the trial excavations did no more than confirm Stenberger's observations concerning the stratigraphy and the thickness of the soil.

Sture Norrby was very young in 1936, but he maintains that he knows the approximate site of the find from what his father told him. Since he began to cultivate the field himself, he has not observed rust traces or iron fragments in any particular area. He was not certain whether any fragments of wood had been brought to the surface in the course of agricultural activities and promised to look out for such traces during future ploughing. However nothing has resulted from his attention.

With Norrby's help an attempt was made to define the site of the find in relation to the main road and the Stora Mästermyr canal (Pl. 31). From the bridge where road no. 140 crosses the canal, 1250 m was measured on the car mileometer while travelling towards Hemse along this road, which follows the course of the canal. At this distance a marked bend in the road was reached, close to the western boundary of the field. Norrby estimated the distance from the canal to the site as about 200 m (not about 300 m, as stated by Jacobsson). Since the map (Pl. 31) was completed the field has been enlarged a little towards the south-west. More than half the plot is still not under cultivation, but it yields some gravel near where the map bears the legend S (= common gravel pit')

No detailed account of the circumstances of the find survives in the documents deposited in ATA. This led me to contact the finder Hugo Kraft of Ålarve, Rone. The information given to me by him and his wife in July 1979 is of interest here: the present account is based on my extensive notes (deposited in ATA).

Hugo Kraft, a farmer born in Björke parish, Jönköping *län* in 1906, moved to Hemse, Gotlands *län* in 1925. His wife Maria, née Eriksson, was born in Rone in 1907 but moved to Hemse in the same year In 1950 the couple moved from Hemse to Ålarve 1[18] and 1[25] in Rone.

Hugo Kraft s account of the circumstances of the find in 1936

Kraft was hired with his tractor to plough for the first time that part of Mästermyr which had been acquired by Emil Norrby of Snoder Sproge. The work was made difficult by sedge tussocks and bad weather

On the first day (the work lasted three or four days) Norrby the landowner was present, following the plough to turn the sods the right way and to assist generally The next day his place was taken by a farmworker on daily wages. Kraft could not remember his name, but he lived in a cottage at Stenbro (see p. 5). The discovery was made during the second day when it rained hard. Kraft described how they began ploughing in the centre of the part of the lot which Norrby planned to cultivate. The furrows ran back and forth between the road (and the adjacent canal) and the south-east boundary of the field. The depth of ploughing was 10 *tum* or 25–30 cm. The area to be cultivated was limited not, according to Kraft, because the soil in the west was inferior but because it had been decided not to cultivate a large area in the first instance ((?)trial cultivation). Kraft also stated that in 1936 much of the reclaimed land in other lots was still not under plough. He had subsequently ploughed other parts of Mästermyr but had never encountered any other 'antiquities either there or elsewhere.

Kraft was shown a sketch map on which the site of the find was marked 300 m from the canal (as stated by Jacobsson) He immediately remarked that this was too far to the southeast. He considered the position indicated by Sture Norrby (based on information from his father) as more likely but thought that it should lie further to the east. The site of Stenberger's excavation, where no traces of the find were discovered, he also considered to be wrong.

The first object to appear was a large and very fragmentary cauldron (?) "of bronze" which was immediately thrown aside as useless. On the return journey the plough-bill caught in the chain which was wrapped round the chest and pulled it up. The chest broke open and its contents became visible. Kraft believed that the chest was found 45–50 cm from the cauldron.

The chest was filled with a "gruel of rust' Kraft did not disturb this 'gruel' very much, but he picked up the steelyard and the large key which he called "the church key' He saw the nodes on these objects and remembers wondering if they were of gold or brass. The next day he picked up the hacksaw and tried it to see whether it could still cut: it produced a scratch on one of the other objects in the find.

At the end of the day he took the steelyard and the key home to show his wife. She thought that the objects should be shown immediately to the representative of the Central Board of National Antiquities, Karl Jacobsson of Alva, and arranged for Hans Norrby of Hemse to drive her to see him that same evening.

Jacobsson is reported to have exclaimed: "Oh, this is something very fine—it is a thousand years old!' When he picked up the objects he laid them on "two sheets of newspaper and carried them in front of him in both hands" When Maria told me this, her husband added, "and I strapped them to the carrier of my bicycle!'

After Jacobsson had made his report, Kraft maintains that two or three gentlemen came from Visby in a car belonging to the late Bengt Hansson of Halldings, Hemse. They sifted the soil and looked for more objects.

*

When I asked Kraft whether he had seen anything lying outside the chest, or any wood which could have not belonged to the broken chest (round timbers or branches, for instance) he answered firmly that he had seen no objects outside the chest other than the cauldron (which had been found first) and no wood fragments. He had not noticed anything else later when ploughing.

When asked if he had seen the fire-grid, which could definitely not have been inside the chest, he answered that he had not seen it and had not heard of this object.

Kraft received 300 Sw kr as a reward from the Central Board of National Antiquities, and shared this with the landowner (who had asked for a share) and with the farm labourer who replaced the landowner on the day of the find. They each received 100 Sw kr

The Krafts also both identified the key which they called the 'church key" with drawings of the large key with faceted nodes of bronze (no. 2) They did not know of any other large key from the find (see notes on the missing large key p. 6)

It has not been possible to confirm the information that two or three gentlemen from Visby excavated on the site after Jacobsson made his report. The people who could have been involved in such investigations were dead by 1979 and my attempts to find notes or diaries have not succeeded.

In August 1981 I discussed the find with Gunnar Norrby headmaster of Lövsta Agricultural College in Romakloster and his sister Dagmar Persson of Puser Fröjel, both children of the former landowner Emil Norrby Gunnar Norrby was not yet at school in 1936, but he had a vivid memory of the find, although naturally enough he did not recall who had taken part in the collection of the find or any subsequent excavations in the following days. His sister Dagmar Persson, was at school and remembers that excavations of long "crosswise" trenches were carried out some time later and that these were left untouched by ploughing for several years. Nothing of importance was found during these excavations. It seems likely that she remembered Stenberger's investigation in the autumn of 1937

All the Norrby children maintain that no part of the find was brought home to Snoder farm. One of them recalls that he was very disappointed that he could not keep any of the objects.

Dagmar Persson knew that the casual worker said by Kraft to have been present on the day of the discovery was called Erik Eriksson, and now lived in the Sudergården old people's home in Burgsvik. A conversation with him on August 29th 1981 however produced no new information: he had only a faint memory of the discovery of a chest and iron objects while ploughing in the fen.

*

It is evident that some of the larger objects were lying outside and adjacent to the tool-chest. The chest is not large enough to have held such items as the cauldrons nos. 19, 23 and 24, the fire-grid, no. 31 and perhaps the largest of the tongs, no. 44. The number of the other heavier tools which could have fitted into the chest depends on how many had complete handles at the time of the deposition.

The detailed examination carried out by me in 1936 when the objects arrived in the State Historical Museum, and before conservation procedures began, revealed that several of the heavy tools (sledge hammers hammers and axes) had traces of wood in the haftholes. These wood fibres are in some cases not visible after conservation. The small size of the chest makes it less likely that all the tools placed there had complete handles. It would also be remarkable if such heavy hafts were not preserved while much thinner handle fragments on smaller objects remain e.g. the key no. 3 the saw no. 42 and the (?) scribing tool no. 97)

It is difficult to determine the proportion of usable tools and of damaged tools and scrap-iron. Of the edge-tools about 30 % have undamaged edges and complete haft-holes or tangs. The cauldrons and the bells may have been incomplete and were certainly not new and this is also the case with the fire-grid and the griddle, which are not only defective but show signs of repair The damage to the steelyard, however could be due to rough handling when it was found.

*

The composition of the find and the proportions of tool types seem to support the interpretation that this was the tool-chest of a farm which needed a good supply of equipment for blacksmiths and carpenters or boatbuilders. The presence of raw iron, damaged objects and scrap suggests that the raw material used for iron work was partly raw iron ingots and pig iron and partly re-used scrap.

The tool-chest, tools and other material from Mästermyr must be regarded as a closed find, but it is not certain that all the objects originally found have been preserved and deposited in the museum. We know that at least one object, the adze no. 64, was first removed as a 'souvenir' by a private person and then handed back to Stenberger in the autumn of 1937 through the intervention of Karl Jacobsson. At the same time Jacobsson handed over two objects, the anvil no. 74 and the trace-ring no. 88 which had been accidentally left behind when Erik Bohrn collected the find.

A rumour that a large key from the find was in private ownership was still circulating in the area in the early 1970s. Erik Nylén, Inspector of Ancient Monuments in Visby reported the matter to me and later undertook investigations, but these proved fruitless.[2]

*

The continued uncertainty as to the original depth of the tool-chest and the stratigraphy of the actual site makes it very difficult to determine how it ended up in this place.

One possibility which has not before been considered is that it was buried at the edge of the fen as a temporary hiding place. Special consideration should perhaps be given to the fact that the small, shallow swamps would dry up more or less completely during warm summers. It is generally accepted that the chest— which was presumably too heavy to carry—and the objects found near it were lost while crossing an ancient waterway that it fell from a capsized boat or perhaps from some vehicle travelling on the ice. Such suggestions can only properly be considered in the light of an examination of the water-levels and conditions at Mästermyr at the time of this supposed accident.

In collaboration with Mårten Stenberger and Gösta Berg a study was made in the 1940s by the State Geologist Fil. Dr Gösta Lundqvist of Stockholm. His material and conclusions are published here in Appendix I.

Since Lundqvist's death in 1967 Gotland's fens have been the subject of new studies, in particularly by Ingemar Påhlsson of Uppsala (1977). However he informs me that there are as yet no new results to add to Lundqvist's investigations. Påhlsson therefore advises the publication of Lundqvist's study as its information is still relevant.

A find in the same area in 1981

A large axe was discovered by Kjell Norrby the son of the landowner Sture Norrby during the potato harvest in September 1981 The site of this find lies to the east of the field where potatoes were grown in 1979 and therefore to the east of the area excavated by Stenberger in 1937 and outside the area investigated by metal detector in 1979 (see above) As the harvesting machine was travelling southwards, and as it is likely that the axe was dragged along for some distance, it is not possible to establish the site of this find in relation to the Stenbro-Hemse road. The depth at which the axe lay (after the area was last ploughed) can be estimated at 20 cm at most, as this is the depth at which the machine normally operates

After that new discovery from the same field, fresh investigations were carried out using a metal detector over an area of c. 8400 m^2 cf. map Pl. 32) On this occasion the work was carried out in my presence by the expert Majvor Östergren at the Central Board of National Antiquities, Gotland division. Even this attempt failed to produce any results.

The axe is of a type not found in the Mästermyr chest found in 1936; it is most similar to the weapon axes Rygh 555 (Rygh 1885) which Petersen dates to the tenth century 1919) in his account 1951) of tool axes no similar examples are mentioned.

Thus it is not at present advisable to group this find together with the Mästermyr discovery of 1936. But the axe and the area where it was found are of interest and it is included as an appendix to the catalogue, with an illustration (Fig. 3)

Sture Norrby gave the axe in to Gotlands Fornsal in December 1981 along with information about where it was found. The above account is based on additional information given over the telephone in February 1982.

---

[2] The correspondence between Per Jacobsson of Lingvide, Havdhem, and Nylén concerning these enquiries is kept in the letter book of the Gotland division of the Central Board of National Antiquities. Among those asked for information in this matter were apparently two daughters of Hugo Kraft, the finder

2. Catalogue

by Greta Arwidsson

Notes on the catalogue

The objects in the find have been given many different sets of numbers, which has made it particularly difficult to produce a systematic account. For the purposes of this publication I have used the numbers in the main catalogue of the State Historical Museum throughout. Where objects have been signed, these are the numbers which occur on them.

A draft description was written by Greta Arwidsson for the museum's catalogue early in 1937 before conservation began. The present account is mainly based on this draft and its accompanying detailed drawings. It has only been necessary in some cases to add information about the condition of the objects after conservation, the objects which arrived in the museum in the autumn of 1937 (see above) are also described. *In the museum's main catalogue the find was given the number 21592* [1]

The subsidiary numbers from the museum catalogue have been used in the present account, and these numbers also appear in the illustrations. *Thus the reference Pl. 16:31 indicates that the fire-grid no. 31 is illustrated in Pl. 16.*

The chest   Pls. 1 and 15: 132, 13–16

Chest of oak with lock and hinges of iron.

The chest is rectangular with a lid curved in cross section and a flat bottom. The bottom is joined to the ends by mortice and tenon joints. The chest is held together by wooden pegs at the ends and sides. The ends and sides are trapezoid and therefore slope inwards at a slight angle. The ends which are made of a slightly thicker scantling than the sides and the bottom, have a rectangular mortice about 4 cm from the lower edge for the tenons of the bottom plank. The lower portion of each end thus forms a raised base.

The ends, sides, bottom and lid each seem to have been made from a single piece of wood. The underside of the lid is hollowed out, leaving an oval, trough-like depression. On either side of the depression the underside of the lid is flat, where the original thickness of the plank has been preserved, this provides a good fit against the upper edges of the end planks.

The sides are pegged to the ends and the bottom and the bottom is joined by mortice and tenon to the ends, a rectangular tenon at each end of the bottom plank fits into a mortice in the ends The details of the construction can best be seen in the illustrations.

The wood seems less carefully dressed on the inside than on the outside. However it is difficult to comment on details of the finish or on any surface treatment of the wood because of its poor condition.

The nature of the damage to the wooden parts of the chest is not easy to determine. About half of one end is missing and there are jagged, elongated holes in the lid and the back. While this damage could have been caused either before or during the deposition of the chest in Mästermyr it is equally possible that it resulted from decay or from rough handling when the chest was discovered. However an oval-shaped hole in the lid seems to have existed in antiquity, as its edges are worn or deliberately smoothed down.

The iron fittings on the chest consisted of a large lock, a long lock-plate and two hinges. The fittings are all fragmentary and were possibly already defective by the time the chest served its last purpose as a container for tools.

The lock (nos. 13–15) of which some parts are preserved on the inside of the front, was a draw-lock of a common type. The bolt consists of a square rod, now damaged and bent at the end, with an expanded disclike central part. Riveted to the disc are the ward plate and three cruciform wards, each 0.5 cm high.

A 47 cm-long lock-plate of iron is nailed to the outside of the chest in front of the lock. The upper edge of the plate (immediately below the top of the chest) and the right-hand edge, show an original straight, clipped finish, the cut corner between these two edges also seems to be original. The other two edges are more or less incomplete. Only eight nails of the original twenty now remain. The nails are turned over on the inside of the wooden panel, they are each about 2.7 cm long. The heads diameter 1.2 cm) are well-made and slightly

---

The descriptions in the museum's main catalogue, which are signed by two members of the museum's staff, are based on the same draft of Greta Arwidsson. The detailed drawings in the draft are omitted from the main catalogue or are copied in summary form.

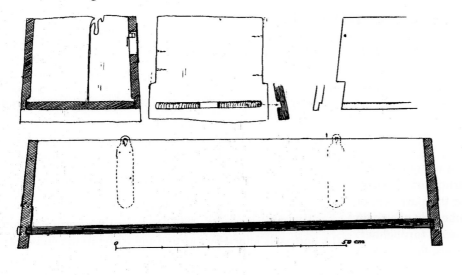

Fig. 1 Details of the construction of the chest (cf pl. 15) Nordiska Museet.

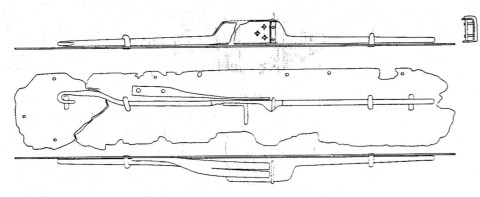

Fig. 2. The chest's lock. Scale 1:4.

domed. The keyhole, now corroded, had one vertical and one horizontal slot set at right angles. Its form indicates a simple thin hooked key of a completely different type from the keys with multi-toothed bits which are included in the find (nos. 2 and 3). Two vertical holes near the ends of the lock-plate may have held staples in which the bolt engaged. On the front of the plate, between the keyhole and the two smaller openings, are two pairs of thin hammered rivets which seem to have served to hold another pair of loops through which the bolt ran.

There were probably two *hinges* (nos. 13–16) each consisting of two iron straps of equal width fitted across the lid and two thirds of the way to the bottom of the back plank. Crosswise wood fibres can be seen on the back of the straps. One end of the strap of the best-preserved hinge is rounded and the other end has a loop. Three nails with domed heads are preserved: the longest is 3.3 cm and indicates the minimum thickness of the original plank. There are holes for another two nails. The other flange of this hinge is incomplete: it has traces of only one nail, and an open hook at one end

which may be fragmentary or may have been damaged by bending. It would probably have been more closed, and would have engaged in the loop of the other half of the hinge. The mount with the closed loop was attached to the back of the chest and the other to the lid.

A fragmentary iron band with two remaining nail heads of the type found elsewhere on the chest and with crosswise wood fibres on the back presumably represents the other hinge.

Chest: sides 86.0–88.5 × 20.5 × 1.8 cm and 87.5–89.5 × 20.9 × 1.8 cm, ends 22.4–26.2 × 1.8–2.5 × 24.2 cm and 21.5–26.3 × 23.8 × 1.8–2.7 cm, lid 88.5 × 24.0 × 3.2 cm.

Iron chain   Pl. 16:17

The chain is made up of twenty-six figure-of-eight shaped links, one oval link and one circular link. The links are welded together and the joins are no longer visible. The figure-of-eight links were pinched together with tongs while hot.

Total length 2.4 m, links 8 7–11 1 cm long; circular link diameter 8.4 cm, rods (square section) 0.8–1.0 cm thick.

It was reported that the chain was wound round the chest when it was pulled up by the plough. It was sufficiently long to have been wound twice round it, but the chain could equally have attached the chest to some larger object, such as some means of transport.

So far as I know no simple Viking Age chain of comparable dimensions has been found in Scandinavia, and it is difficult to identify its original purpose. Links of a similar size have been found both in cauldron-chains and chains used as harnesses for carts and other vehicles (Stolpe and Arne 1912, Vendel I V and XI Arwidsson 1954 and 1977 Almgren 1946) However this chain is considerably longer and heavier than those used for these purposes. The complete cauldron-chain from the Oseberg ship burial does have a total length of about 2 m, but this measurement also includes the two suspension hooks. The chain from Sutton Hoo, a uniquely fine example of metal-work, is much longer (3 75 m) and very strong (Petersen 1951 409· Bruce-Mitford 1972, fig. 16–17)

Steelyard   Pls. 2 and 16:1

Steelyard of iron and bronze consisting of an iron bar of generally round section with a small bronze disc at one end. A decorated cylindrical mount, 3.5 cm from the hook end of the bar and two faceted nodes are also of bronze. There are no visible gradations on the bar

The hook is suspended from a U-shaped shackle damaged near the rivet), and consists of a suspension loop, an expanded middle section with a bronze node above and below it, and a flat hook which terminates in a pointed beak. The middle section is made up of four twisted rods surrounding a cylindrical ring.

The weight takes the form of an irregular double cone with a wrought, closed suspension loop. It is likely that the small flat ring with a small perforated projection belongs to the weight, although the connecting link between the two is missing.

Two large flat rings were also found, one of which is still attached to a U-shaped shackle closed by a rivet just in front of the hook. About 1 cm further along is another such crosswise rivet which could have secured another shackle in which the second, loose, ring could have been suspended.

Ornament of various kinds occurs on the following parts of the steelyard:

a the bronze nodes on the hook: four punched ring-and-dot motifs are set together on the rhomboid facets one on the triangular facets However on the lower node, two opposite sides have animal head-like ornaments

b the lower flat part of the hook. along the edges of one side are punched triangular impressions the other side was probably undecorated.

c the larger flat rings. on both sides are small triangular impressions (like those on the hook)

d) the cylindrical bronze mount on the bar· along each edge there is a row of ring-and-dot motifs between beaded borders.

e the weight: at the base of the upper cone a row of triangular impressions set closely together· on its surface some irregular and perhaps worn impressions of a similar design.

Length of hook 10.3 cm. Rings diameter 2.3 cm, 5.0 cm (the loose ring) and 5.5 cm, thickness 1.0, 2.0 and 1.5 mm. Bar length 35.3 cm, diameter (round end) 0.8–0.5 cm, (square end) 0.8–0.6 cm. Weight, before conservation 311 g.

Keys lock parts and pad-locks

Key of bronze and iron   Pls 4 and 19:2

Key with a four-toothed bit set at right angles to the shank. The upper part of the shank is spool-shaped and consists of eight twisted iron rods a square collar and a faceted node of bronze. The rods are twisted alternately to the right and the left, internally they are supported by a round iron disc; a bronze strip only half of which is preserved, encircles the widest part. Only a short stub remains of the key's suspension loop. There are no traces of ornament.

Total length 21.4 cm, bit length 8.6 cm, thickness 0.8 cm.

Key of iron with wooden handle   Pls. 4 and 19:3

Key with a three-toothed bit set at a right angle to the shaft. It is made from a square iron rod fitted into a wooden handle. The wood has been identified as ash (see Appendix III) The original form of the handle cannot be determined.

Present length 19.6 m, of which the wood fragments cover 9.8 cm, bit length 9 cm, thickness 0.3 cm.

Lock-plate of iron   Pl. 19:4

Sheet-iron lock-plate of irregular rectangular shape. It has four pins or rivet holes and the central part of one side is turned up to form a rim 0.7 m high. The clipped edges of the plate are original. There is a row of rectangular holes (in which the teeth of the key fitted) in the

middle of the plate. No wood fragments were observed before conservation.
9.6 × 4.5 cm. Thickness of plate 0.15 cm.

Lock-plate of iron   Pl. 19:5
Fragmentary lock-plate with only one original edge. In this edge and the opposite, damaged, edge there are two nail or rivet holes. There is the flat head of a pin or rivet near the row of keyholes There are two separate rows of keyholes one with three rectangular holes—apparently not in line—and the other with two only partly preserved rectangular openings. The keyholes in the two groups are of different sizes. No wood fragments were observed before conservation.
7.3 × 5.2 cm, thickness of plate 0.2 cm.

Lock-spring of iron   Pl. 19:6
Incomplete lock-spring with only one of the original three tongues preserved. In the middle there is a rivet hole.
15 1 × 2.4 × 0.3 cm.

Lock-spring of iron   Pl. 19:7
Lock-spring with three tongues, one of which is broken. In the middle there is a rivet hole. The tapering bolt is probably incomplete.
10.1 × 3 1 × 0.2 cm.

Lock-spring of iron   Pl. 19:8
Iron sheet irregularly tongued at one end, this end is turned back and hammered down. The other end is turned round an oval ring of round section.
10.5 × 2.7 × 0.3 cm, ring 5 1 × 3.9 × 0.5 cm.

(?)Lock-spring blank of iron   Pl. 19:9
Similar to no. 8, it has a tongued end, turned back and hammered down. At the opposite end the sheet tapers and is turned round a ring of round section.
9.4 × 1 9 × 0.2 cm, ring, diameter 3:7 cm, thickness 0.4 cm.

Padlock of iron with brass solder   Pls. 5 and 19·10
Padlock in two parts, with the bottom plate missing. There are clear traces of a yellow metal solder—(?)brass—in the joins between the plates. One of the short sides has a cylindrical socket in which the staple is engaged. Each short side is decorated with three S-twisted iron rods. The keyhole is T-shaped. There are three springs
4.5 × 3.0 × 2.2 cm, shackle height 2.3 cm, thickness of rod 0.4 cm, thickness of plate about 0.1 cm.

Padlock of iron   Pls. 5 and 19:11
Incomplete padlock similar to no. 10 (above) although slightly smaller The staple, part of the keyhole side and part of the bottom are missing. Only one spring remains intact. The decoration is similar to that on padlock no. 10, except that the rods are Z-twisted.
3.0 × 2.9 × 3.6 cm, thickness of plate 0.1–0.2 cm.

Padlock of iron   Pls 5 and 19:12
Incomplete padlock of the same type as nos. 10–11 (above) The staple and socket are missing as well as most of the keyhole side and the bottom. No springs remain. It is decorated with at least four Z-twisted rods.
2.8 × 2.2 × 2.6 cm, thickness of plate about 0.1 cm.

Cauldrons (?)bucket and griddle

Griddle with rim of sheet-iron   Pls. 6 and 24:18
Round disc with up-turned rim and an irregular triangular hole in the middle. It is incomplete: more than a third of the rim and a portion of the bottom are missing. Part of the rim has been secondarily bent inwards The griddle was repaired in antiquity with a triangular patch, riveted on with at least ten rivets. The patch is now partly detached.
Diameter 22.3 cm, thickness of plate 0.3–0.4 cm.

Cauldron of copper alloy   Pls. 11 and 24:19
The almost cylindrical cauldron is made from four separate sheets joined together by overlapping and stitching' the edge of one sheet was inserted alternately over and under flaps cut at the edge of the adjoining sheet and secured by soldering. One sheet forms the bottom, two sheets make up the walls and the fourth is a 3.2 cm-wide strip lining the rim. This strip is thicker than the other sheets especially along the upper edge. It was apparently lengthened with a smaller piece next to one of the handle attachments, and reinforced there by a bronze sheet folded over the rim. The bottom was probably slightly convex. The handle attachments consist of a circular iron plate and a ring-loop. Both are now broken off and one is fragmentary The remains of an older attachment of copper alloy are probably preserved underneath the iron rivet of one of the iron handle attachments (see detailed drawing)
The cauldron is very fragmentary and battered. Old patches secured by numerous rivets can be seen in at least eleven places.
Before conservation the cauldron had a deposit of soot on the outside and a large amount of rust on the inside as well as another deposit, possibly of food remains.

Diameter about 26 cm, height 13.8 cm, thickness of plate 0.2 cm.

Handle of iron   Pls. 10 and 24:20
The handle possibly belongs to the cauldron no. 19 (see above). It is made from a flat rod of rectangular section and has open hooks at the ends. Its curvature has been exaggerated by bending and the distance between the hooks (outside measurement) is now only about 24.4 cm.
Length 24.4 cm, height 16.0 cm, rod width 1.2 cm, thickness 0.4 cm.

(?)Bucket mount of iron   Pl. 25:21
Three pieces of a wide iron band, one edge of which is turned over. This was probably the rim mount of a (?)wooden bucket, with the remains of a riveted handle attachment. The longest piece is made up of two sheets joined together by a vertical row of rivets. A roughly rectangular mount, which clearly ends in a damaged loop just above the turned edge, is attached by rivets to the joined bands.

A rivet-hole about 4 cm from the upper edge of the other portion of the band suggests the position of the second handle attachment, there are also traces of rust here. At the lower edge of the band at least one rivet-hole can be distinguished.
Band, width 9.9 cm, total length about 113 cm (70   23 + 20 cm) thickness of plate about 0.2 cm.

Handle of iron   Pls 10 and 24:22
Iron handle, possibly associated with the mount no. 21 (see above) It is made from a broad, flat iron rod with an open hook at each end. Before conservation one of the hooks retained a fragment of the loop to which the handle had been attached. This loop seemed to be of the same dimensions and appearance as the loop which is attached to the iron mount no. 21 The distance between the hooks outside measurement) is 38 cm, but the curvature of the handle has been exaggerated by bending.
Width 2.3 cm, thickness 0.20–0.35 cm, length 38 cm, height 18.6 cm.

Copper alloy cauldron
with iron handle   Pls. 11 and 24:23–24
Large copper alloy cauldron with a wide iron band round the rim. The walls consist of six bronze sheets of different widths which are joined together by overlapping and stitching' and hammered to an iron band 4.3 cm wide at the top. The copper alloy sheets are turned over the upper edge of the iron band at the rim and cut off on the outside 0.2–0.3 cm below the rim.

The sides are straight and taper slightly towards the bottom, which was probably slightly convex.

The iron band was made in two halves and riveted together with one rivet at each join. The handle is made from an iron rod of rectangular section and has an open hook at each end. There are traces of the iron handle attachments which were apparently oval, the loops are broken off.

The cauldron is very battered and partly damaged. One side is split right down to the bottom and the wall is partly torn away from the bottom. It had been repaired with several riveted patches. There are thick layers of soot on the outside.
Diameter of bottom about 49 cm, height of side 20.5 cm, thickness of copper alloy sheet about 0.05 cm. Iron band width 4.3 cm, thickness 0.4 cm. Handle attachments about 4.6 × 5.6 cm. Handle length 48 cm, height 25 cm, rod width 1.2 cm, thickness 0.7 cm.

Cauldron fragment
of sheet-iron   Pls 10 and 25: unnumbered
Round, slightly dished bottom plate, to which the sides were riveted. Eight rivet-heads remain in the bottom plate along with traces of the side plates, which overlapped the bottom by about 1.5 cm. The fragmentary condition of this object makes it impossible to speculate on how many plates went to make up the sides of the cauldron.
Diameter 10.5–11.2 cm, thickness of plate about 0.15 cm.

Fragment of (?)handle of iron   Pl. 25:25
Fragment of a (?)bent handle, consisting of an iron rod tapering towards one end.
15.2 × 1.0–1.3 × 0.1 cm.

Three bells   Pls 5 and 17:26–28 + 29–30)

The bells were made of sheet-iron. All three are of the same shape and construction, and two still retain their double clappers. A loose pair of clappers presumably belonged to the third bell.

Each bell is made from a plate, cut to shape and folded to form a truncated pyramid and riveted with rows of eight or nine rivets down the middle of two facing sides (see reconstruction Pl. 17)

The suspension loops are iron strips with a slight central ridge and up-turned edges. At the ends the strips are clipped to triangular points which overlapped onto two sides of the bells and were secured by rivets

The drop-shaped *clappers* are all of the same size and shape. The tapering upper part is turned over to form an elongated loop. Rings made from rods of round section form the connecting links between each pair of clappers and the shackle which protrudes from the top of the inside of the bells. The clappers must have been attached before the bells were riveted together

Even the best-preserved of the bells no. 26, lacks its original lower edge and has many holes in its sides. When one of the sides was pushed in, the sheet-metal was split at one corner along almost its entire length The inside is covered with green verdigris from an original copper alloy coating.

Bell no. 27 is very fragmentary and was assembled during conservation from two larger fragments part of the lower edge is preserved. The clappers have rusted together Traces of copper alloy coating can be observed on both the outside and the inside of this bell.

Bell no. 28 is very damaged and fragmentary· even the shackle is bent and broken away on one side. Possible traces of copper alloy coating can be observed on the inside only The clappers are missing, along with the connecting ring from which they were suspended. The clappers nos. 29–30, which have been catalogued separately very probably belong to this bell.

At one place on the inside there is a small piece of (?)lead. A similar piece of (?)lead is attached to a small fragment of sheet-iron, which was therefore probably part of one of the bells.

No. 26: height 22.5 cm, lower edge 17.5 × 14.1 cm, top surface 6.1 × 4.1 cm, thickness of plate 0.2 cm, clappers length about 18 cm, maximum diameter 1.3 cm.

No. 27· height 25.9 cm, width of complete side at the lower edge 15.5 cm, top surface 6.7 × 4.0 cm, thickness of plate 0.2–0.3 cm; clappers length about 17 cm, maximum diameter 1.2 cm.

No. 28. height 25 9 cm, width of the complete side at the lower edge 15.5 cm, top surface 5 1 × 4.1 cm, thickness of plate 0.2 cm.

Nos. 29–30: clappers from (?)no. 28. Length 20.6–20.7 cm, diameter 0.5–0.9 cm.

Fire-grid of iron   Pls. 3 and 16:31

A square iron grid, originally suspended from four chains attached to a swivel-loop.

The frame of the grid is made from straight iron strips, riveted at each corner and bent at a near right angle along the middle to form a raised edge. The chains would probably have been attached to forged hooks at the ends of the strips (see detailed drawing) One of these hooks had secondarily been replaced by an Ωshaped loop. The grid is made of ten parallel iron

rods riveted to the horizontal parts of the frame. Across the middle of these rods lie two iron bands, one above and one below and joined together by single rivets in the space between the rods.

The chains are made of straight links of varying lengths These have either open or closed loops at both ends, the loop at one end set approximately at right angles to the loop at the other end. The rods from which the links are made have rectangular sections

The chains are attached at the top to an iron plate with four hooked arms. The rod of the swivel-loop passes through a hole in the centre of the plate. A large hook, bent over at the upper end, is attached to this loop.

The fire-grid is partly defective and was also repaired in antiquity One of the rods is missing and only half of another survives. One chain is also missing. Apart from the secondary loop in one corner (see above) the frame had been repaired with a small riveted patch, and the frame is now broken in this place. The double iron bands across the grid are broken and partly incomplete.

Frame about 50 × 50 cm, strip width 0.45 cm, thickness 0.25 cm, grid rods 49.0 × 1.2 × 0.3–0.5 cm. Chain links about 0.6–0.7 cm, total length of each chain about 42 cm. Swivel. four-armed plate about 16 × 9 cm, thickness 0.3 cm, hook 10.3 × 1.5 × 0.7 cm, the open part of the hook maximum width 1.5 cm.

Note During conservation an iron wire was put round the outside of the grid to strengthen it.

Carpenters and (?)blacksmiths ıron tools

Two files   Pls. 7 and 22.32–33
Files of rectangular section. The larger file is cut on all four faces, one being markedly finer than the others. The smaller file is cut on three faces, of which two are fine and the third rather coarser The tangs show no traces of wood.
No. 32. 21.6 × 0.8–1 1 × 0.5–0.9 cm.
No. 33 16.9 × 0.5–1.0 × 0.4–0.6 cm.

Round file   Pl. 7:34
Strongly tapering tang of square section. The cut surface of the file covers about two thirds of the circumference. The tang shows no traces of wood.
15 1 × 0.4–0.7 cm.

File   Pl. 23:35
File of rectangular section with coarse-cut surfaces on all four faces (5 cuts per cm) The point is very thin and

has been damaged by bending. No visible traces of wood.
Overall length 16.1 length of cut section 7.8 cm, tang 8.3 cm, maximum width 0.9 cm, thickness 0.5 cm.

Rasp Pl. 23:37
Coarse rasp of rectangular section and offset tang. Only one face is cut (4 cuts per cm)
Before conservation there were a few traces of wood on the tang.
Overall length 27 7 cm, tang 8.6 cm, width 1.5–1.0 cm, thickness 0.3–0.6 cm.

Rasp Pls. 7 and 23:38
Similar to no. 37 (see above) but much smaller Only one face is cut (about 11 cuts per cm); the cut area is divided in half by a lengthwise groove.
Overall length 12.5 cm, tang 4.5 cm, width 0.9 cm, thickness 0.5 cm.

Knife Pl. 26:39
Knife with a long, straight tang and short blade; the back of the blade is straight and the cutting edge curved with a pointed angle between blade and tang. The back of the blade has a central ridge.
17.6 × 1.8 × 0.8 cm.

(?)Knife blade Pl. 29:40
Fragmentary iron blade with straight back and cutting edge, broken off at the wider end (no trace of a tang) Part of the cutting edge is serrated. The blade is damaged by bending and is torn in one place.
7.5 × 1 1 × 0.4.

Saw with wooden handle Pls. 14 and 27:42
Broad hand-saw with teeth filed from opposite sides of the blade in groups of four The straight back and edge of the knife-like blade are parallel for most of its length, but converge towards the point, the back showing the most pronounced curvature. The well-preserved handle is of ash, probably a piece of a branch, and is damaged at the end where the point of the tang is bent at right angles to the blade.
61.4 × 4.8 × 0.4 cm; handle 12.5 × 3.4 cm.

Six spoon-augers Pls. 13 and 28:46–51
The six boring-bits are of different sizes but their form is the same: they have spoon-shaped blades, rounded or faceted octagonal shanks and short pointed tangs of rectangular section. Four augers (nos 46–49) retain an iron collar which encircled a now decayed wooden handle.

Apart from minor damage, the augers are well preserved. Before conservation they were so rusty that the collars went unnoticed.
No. 46: 44.2 × 1.8 × 1.2 cm, spoon length 10.1 cm, width 1 7 cm, collar diameter 3.4 cm.
No. 47· 37.0 × 1.5 × 2.1 cm, spoon length about 8.5 cm, width 2.9 cm, collar diameter 3.2 cm.
Before conservation this auger was rusted together with a round iron object 37.0 cm long and 1.5 cm in diameter and another smaller iron object 6.1 cm long (see nos. 52 and 125).
No. 48: 37.0 (the points at both ends are broken) × 1.3 × 1.8 cm, spoon present length 8.1 cm, width 1 9 cm, collar diameter 3.0 cm.
No. 49: 34.8 × 1.2 × 1.8 cm, spoon length 8.0 cm, width 1.9 cm; collar diameter 2.7 × 4.3 cm.
No. 50: 24.4 × 1.0 × 1.4 cm, spoon length 4.8 cm, width 1.4 cm.
No. 51 16.6 × 0.5 × 0.7 cm, spoon length 2.2 cm, width 0.7 cm.

Draw-knife Pls. 13 and 27:54
Band-shaped draw-knife with curved, sharp-edged blade. The tangs curve inwards at right angles to the plane of the blade and their ends are bent outwards No traces of the wooden handle remain.
6.7 × 7.8 cm, blade width 1.2 cm, maximum thickness 0.4 cm.

?)Draw-knife fragment Pl. 28:55
Fragment consisting of a curved blade with a sharp edge along one side and a slightly curved tang. A second tang may have been broken off along with part of the blade. The fracture reveals the triangular section of the blade.
12.2 × 1.5 × 0.5 cm.

Moulding-iron Pls. 13 and 27:57
Tool used to produce mouldings on wooden objects On either side of the central support the edge is profiled. The tangs are curved and bend outwards at the ends. One tang is incomplete.
8.1 × 9.2 × 0.3 cm, width of blade at the support 1.5 cm, tangs width 0.6 cm, thickness 0.4 cm.

Gouge Pl. 28:58
Curved blade of uniform width with square cutting edge and straight tang of rectangular section. The edge is damaged.
16.4 × 0.9 × 0.6 cm.

Note. It is tentatively suggested that this tool was used in coopering, to cut the channel which took the bottom of the barrel or cask (see Fig. 5:a)

Chisel   Pls. 12 and 26:59
Chisel with a broad splayed cutting edge and a straight
shaft with faceted edges which continues as a straight
tang of approximately square section. The end of the
tang is slightly bent to one side and is hammered to a
knob similar to a rivet-head.
26.0 × 4.7 × 0.9 cm.

Axe   Pls. 12 and 26:61
Axe with almost straight top contour and two flanges
extending downwards on each side of the semi-oval
haft-hole. The cutting edge of the blade has rusted
away
Length 22.0 cm, width at cutting edge 6.7 cm, butt 2.0
× 4.5 cm. At the narrowest point the width is 2.3 cm,
weight 752 g.

Axe   Pls. 12 and 26:62
Similar to no. 61 (see above) but this axe originally had
a more flared edge ('bearded' axe). The damaged part
of the edge has been bent over and hammered down
firmly
15.0 × 4.6 × 2.9 cm, butt 3.0 × 2.3 cm, weight 463 g.

Adze   Pls. 12 and 26:63
T-shaped adze with a broad, slightly curved cutting
edge. The butt has a rectangular striking face and a tip
which points downwards. There are downward-point-
ing flanges on each side of the oval haft-hole. The adze
is curved from butt to cutting edge. The cutting edge is
damaged.
19.8 × 17.0 × 1 7 cm, weight 719 g.

Adze   Pls. 12 and 26:64
Similar to no. 63 (see above) but the cutting edge is
slightly curved and unusually narrow The cutting edge
is damaged.
15.5 × 5.9 × 1.4 cm, striking face of peen 1.9 × 2.5 cm;
weight 272 g.

Blacksmiths iron tools

Hammer   Pls. 6 and 20:65
Hammer with thin peen: the bottom contour is almost
straight and the top comprises two slightly curved
planes which meet in a point at the haft-hole. The hole
retains traces of a wooden haft.
16.6 × 2.9 × 3.8 cm, striking face 2.5 × 3.6 cm, weight
724 g.

Hammer   Pls. 6 and 21:66
The surface of the hammer is rough, it is faceted with

partly concave sides. One end widens to a rounded
head with a domed, convex striking face, while the
rectangular striking face at the other end is almost flat.
The haft-hole is off-centre. There are traces of the
wooden haft.
21.0 × 2.9 × 2.8 cm, weight 602 g.

Hammer   Pls. 6 and 21:67
The haft-hole on this hammer is closer to the peen than
to the striking face. There were no traces of wood.
14.5 × 2.6 × 2.6 cm, weight 407 g.

Hammer (stretching hammer)   Pls. 8 and 20:68
The hammer has a rectangular haft-hole near the
rounded butt, a slightly faceted head of uniform width
and a round, slightly domed and burred striking face.
There are perhaps some traces of wood in the haft-hole.
14.8 × 3.0 × 2.1 cm, weight 481 g.

Sledge hammer   Pls. 6 and 20:69
The sledge hammer has a straight bottom and an angled
top with the point over the haft-hole. The upper surface
has a slight central ridge. The haft-hole retains traces of
the wooden haft.
24.5 × 5.6 × 5.6 cm, weight 3370 g.

Sledge hammer   Pls. 6 and 21·70
The bottom of the head is slightly dished, the upper
surface is like that described above (no. 69) but is not
ridged. The haft-hole retains traces of the wooden haft.
21.3 × 3.8 × 5.0 cm, weight 1862 g.

Sledge hammer   Pls 6 and 21·71
The head tapers a little towards the butt and the peen is
thinner towards the end. The top contour is slightly
S-shaped. The striking face of the butt is strongly burred. There are traces of the wooden haft in the oval
haft-hole.
19.7 × 3.9–4.8 × 3 7 cm, weight 1596 h.

Tongs   Pl. 22:43
Small tongs with flat jaws. Most of the shanks are
missing.
6.1 × 5.9 × up to 0.2 cm, shanks width 1.0 cm, thickness 0.15 cm, jaws maximum width 1.0 cm.

Smithing tongs   Pls. 7 and 22:44
Well-preserved large tongs with flat jaws. The shanks
have round sections and the other parts rectangular
sections.
56.0 × 10.0 × 3.2 cm, shanks length 20.5 cm, thickness
about 1.5 cm, jaws maximum width 3.0 cm.

Hack-saw of iron   Pls. 7 and 22:36
The tool has two parts. a frame of uniform width which continues to form a tapering tang, and a straight, fine-toothed saw-blade, riveted at one end to the front of the frame and at the other end to the point where the tang begins The join between the front of the frame and the saw-blade has been further strengthened by flattening the frame and bending round the blade of the flattened portion. Frame, tang and blade are flat and of rectangular section. The saw-blade is slightly damaged.
Total length 24.0 cm, total height 3.6 cm; frame width 0.6–0.8 cm, maximum thickness 0.25 cm, blade width 0.7–1.0 cm, thickness 0.15 cm.

Saw-blade of iron with coarse teeth   Pls. 14 and 26:41
The teeth are set alternately to the right and left. The saw-toothed edge is slightly curved and the blade, which is of almost uniform width, continues in a strongly tapering tang. There are no traces of wood on the tang. The tip of the blade is broken off.
34.5 × 2.0 × 0.4 cm.

Plate-shears   Pls. 6 and 22:45
The blades are not sharpened and the shanks are curved. The blades and lower parts of the shanks have rectangular sections, while the upper parts of the shanks have plano-convex sections.
Length 46.7 cm, blades maximum length 1.8 cm, thickness 0.4 cm, shanks maximum width 2.2 cm, thickness 1.0 cm.

Cold drill   Pl. 23:52
The cold drill consists of a cylindrical rod, drilled at one end to a tube about 4 cm long. It tapers slightly at the other end where there is a slightly domed striking face.
36.9 × 1.4 cm; striking face diameter 1.6 cm.

Polishing iron   Pl. 23:53
Tool used to polish soldered joints. It consists of a round iron rod, bent at right angles at one end, while the other end is straight and forged to a narrow edge.
Length 30.0 cm, diameter 0.6 cm, width at edge 0.4 cm.

Anvil   Pls. 9 and 21:72
Anvil of iron, the narrow base has a slightly concave surface, while the striking face is slightly convex. The shape is roughly but irregularly square.
7.8 × 4.0 × 3.0 cm.

Anvil   Pls. 9 and 20:73
Anvil of iron, tapering towards the base. The top and bottom faces are both slightly concave. The long sides are flat, the narrow sides curved.
5.9 × 4.0 × 2.1 cm.

Anvil   Pls. 9 and 20:74
Anvil of iron, presumably used for lighter work. The shape is roughly cylindrical, but very irregular On two opposite sides there are deep depressions. One side may be damaged.
5.2–6.2 × 4.2 cm.

Anvil (beak-iron)   Pls. 8 and 21·75
Beak-iron, it is angular with tapering beak and square section. The foot tapers to a point and the section is circular
Beak length 11.9 cm, width at base 2.7 cm, thickness up to 3.0 cm, foot length 12.6 cm, maximum thickness 2.4 cm.

Anvil (beak-iron)   Pl. 21·76
Small beak-iron. A pointed foot of circular section projects from the centre of the striking face. One half of the striking face is of rectangular section and the other half of circular section.
3.4 × 1.0 × 0.8 cm, foot length 2.2 cm.

Underlay   Pls. 8 and 23·77
This object is made from a coarse iron bar of rectangular section, bent to the shape of an open oval ring. It was perhaps used as an underlay during riveting.
9.2 × 1.8 × 6.2 cm, bar 2.8 × 1 7 cm.

Note Before conservation there were traces of wood from the chest on one side and two smaller (?) iron fragments were rusted to the ring.

Underlay   Pls. 8 and 23·78
Similar to no. 77 but smaller It is made from a coarse bar of nearly square section with rounded edges. The bar was bent to form an open oval ring.
4.9 × 3.8 × 1.6 cm, bar thickness 1.0 cm.

Punching block or uncompleted draw plate   Pl. 23·79
An iron bar cut at both ends and slightly curved lengthwise. Along the middle of the bar is a single row of twenty-two round-bottomed holes with traces of what may have been another hole at one end. Seven holes have been struck so hard that the punch perforated the bar
16.4 × 1.2 × 0.4 cm.

Punching block or uncompleted draw plate   Pl. 23:80
A flat iron bar which tapers at both ends. Twenty-six holes six of which perforate the bar are placed in two irregular rows.
13 7 × 1.2 × 0.3 cm.

(?) Draw plate blank   Pl. 23:81
Similar to nos. 79–80 but without punch marks.
12.9 × 1 1 × 0.4 cm.

Dölley   Pl. 23:82
A bar of round section, hollow at one end.
10.1 × 1.5 cm, striking face 2.2 cm.

The tool was used during riveting, serving to hold firm the
members of wood which were to be joined, as for instance
when riveting the planks of a boat.

Tool   Pl. 29:83
(?) Chisel. A curved square rod with one end forged to a
thin but unsharpened edge, and the other turned over to
form an open loop parallel to the edge.
15.4 × 0.9 × 1.2 cm.

Stamp punch   Pl. 22:84
A square rod which thickens towards the striking face.
The surface of the stamp, which is much damaged by
wear and rusting, has an ornament of hour-glass shape.
It is no longer possible to verify this description.
7.5 × 0.4–0.8 × 0.4–0.7 cm, striking face diameter 0.9
cm.

Stamping pad of lead   Pls. 10 and 22:85
An irregularly shaped pad of lead: on both sides there
are impressions which may have been made by the
stamp no. 84, as well as of circles and small holes The
hour-glass ornament is sometimes arranged in irregular
ribbon-like rows.
5.9 × 5.0 × 0.4 cm.

Note The impressions in the lead show three dots at each corner of
the triangles which make up the motif. These dots could not be seen
on the stamp either before or after conservation.

Nail-making iron   Pls. 12 and 23:86
The nail-making iron is made from a thick rectangular
bar with a forged faceted handle at one end. Along the
centre are five holes, four nearly conical and one cylindrical.
22.9 × 1.9–3.8 × 2.1 cm. The maximum and minimum
diameter of the conical holes varies. maximum 0.8–1 1
cm, minimum 0.6–1.0 cm, the cylindrical hole diameter
1 1 cm.

Other tools and objects

Scraper or ash-rake   Pl. 29:60
Iron rod handle with a transverse rectangular plate
secured by two rivets.
Length 26.9 cm, plate 9.5 × 5.4 × 0.1–0.2 cm.

Two trace-rings of iron   Pls. 4 and 18.87–88
Rings for fastening traces to the axle-tree of a cart (see
Almgren 1946) The rings are made from an iron rod,
part of which is hammered flat and shaped into a large
loop: the outside edge is thinner than the inside edge.
The ends of the rod are twisted to form a shank which
ends in a smaller round loop in the same plane as the
large loop.
    No. 87· length 22.5 cm, large loop diameter 10.7 cm,
small loop diameter 4.5 cm, thickness 1.4 cm.
    No. 88: length 23.4 cm, large loop diameter 10.0 cm,
small loop diameter 4.3 cm, thickness 1.6 cm.

Two trace-rings of iron   Pls. 4 and 18:89–90
Rings for fastening traces to the axle-tree of a cart.
Each ring is made from a single rod and consists of a
larger flat loop and a smaller loop of circular section.
When no. 89 was originally catalogued and drawn, a
small S-shaped iron rod = Pl. 30:125 b was attached to
the smaller loop.
    No. 89: length 14.0 cm, large loop diameter 11.2 cm,
thickness large loop 0.9 cm, small loop 1.2 cm.
    No. 90: length 13.6 cm, large loop diameter 11 1 cm,
thickness large loop 0.9 cm, small loop 1 1 cm.

Round disc of iron   Pl. 18:91
Disc with a squarish hole in the middle and a sharp edge
all the way round.
Diameter 10.2 cm, thickness at the hole 0.5 cm, at the
edge 0.05 cm, hole 1.5×1.6 cm.

*Two tripod stands and part
of a (?)tripod stand* of iron   Pls. 9 and 29:92, 93 125 d
The tripod stands may have served to support hot crucibles. The end of each leg is bent over at right angles to
form a tapering pointed foot. The stands were made
from iron rods of square section.
    No 125 d is perhaps part of a tripod stand which was
similar to nos. 92–93 but heavier Only one leg remains.
it is bent at the end to form a foot. It has been suggested
that this fragment instead could be the end part of a
sickle.
No. 92: 11.5 × 8.8 × 2.0 cm.
No. 93 11.8 × 9.2 × 1.8 cm.
No. 125 d. 7.5 × 1 7–2.5 × 1 7 cm.

Awl of iron   Pl. 29:94
Round awl, tapering to a fine point, with a tang of
rectangular section.
13.0 × 1 1–0.7 × 0.4 cm.

Object of iron   Pl. 29:95
Rod of rectangular section tapering to points at both

ends. One end is slightly and evenly curved, while the other is more curved and possibly damaged.
10.6 × 0.5 × 0.4 cm.

Tool of unknown use with
wooden handle   Pls. 14 and 29:96
Two short blunt iron shanks with a long thin tang which apparently extends the whole length of the well-finished spruce handle. The section of the handle is almost circular
12.8 × 2.4 cm; handle length 12.6, diameter 2.3–2.4 cm.

(?)Scribing tool of iron with
wooden handle   Pls. 14 and 27:97
One side of the iron is finely serrated from the marked spur just below the wooden handle to the (possibly damaged) tip. The tang probably extends the whole length of the handle. At the end of the handle is a groove cutting in from the circumference to just past the centre. The wood is well-polished ash and the handle has a rounded oval section.
Total length 13.1 cm; visible part of iron 3.3 × 1 1 × 0.4 cm, handle 9.8 × 1.8–2.4 cm.

Four rings (collars of iron   Pl. 28:98–101
It is likely that these collars belong to the handles of the spoon-augers (nos. 46–51) Three collars are open and one (no. 100) is closed. Nos. 98 and 99 are almost identical in size and have triangular sections.
No. 98: 3.5 × 2.8 × 1 1 cm.
No. 99: 3.6 × 2.6 × 1.4 cm.
No. 100: 3.3 × 3.3 × 0.8 cm.
No. 101 3.2 × 2.8 × 1.0 cm.

Spatula of iron   Pl. 29:102
Rounded oval flat disc with a very thin tang of rectangular section.
15.0 × 1.5 × 0.3 cm.

U-shaped shackle of iron   Pl. 28:103
The ends of the shackle are broadened and pierced to take the missing bolt. Before conservation the shackle was rusted to the concave side of the cauldron fragment Pl. 25**
33.3 × 2.0 cm, rod thickness 0.6 cm.

Tool of iron   Pl. 20:104
Tool of unknown use. The thinner end has a striking face while the other is slightly concave. The tool is of irregular square section with rounded edges.
15.0 × 3.0–4.0 × 1.5–2.5 cm.

Part of coarse tool of iron   Pl. 27 105
(?)Chisel. Rectangular iron bar the narrow sides flat, the broad sides irregularly concave. The preserved end has a flat striking face, which is slightly burred, there is an irregular fracture at the other end. The section is for the most part octagonal as the edges have been bevelled.
16.0 ×3.0 × 2.7 cm.

Two elongated iron bars   Pls. 14 and 22.110– 11
The bars are of varying width and thickness, and their ends are fractured or damaged. Hallinder 1978 45) has referred to these as currency bars
No. 110: 51.0 × 4.6–2.8 × 1.0–0.5 cm, weight 906 g.
No. 111 48.5 × 4.4–3.0 × 1.0–0.3 cm, weight 872 g.

Slate whetstone or blank   Pl. 27·122
A rough piece of irregular rectangular section. One end is cut obliquely and the other is broken and splintered.
36.6 × 3.5 × 1.0–1.5 cm.

Slate whetstone   Pls. 13 and 27 123
Whetstone of grey slate. Three faces are ground fairly smooth while one broad face shows very irregular grinding marks. One narrow face has a shallow groove and fine scoring. The whetstone is broken at both ends.
15.4 × 1.3 × 1 1 cm.

Indeterminate objects and fragments

Iron object   Pl. 27·56
The use of this object is unknown. A central part forms a semi-circular channel, tapering symmetrically at both ends where two narrow shanks, terminating in points are bent over almost at right angles to the central part. There is some damage to the edge of the channel.
Length 18.0 cm, maximum width 1.9 cm, depth of channel 1.2 cm, shanks length 6.4 cm and 6.6 cm.

Object of iron   Pl. 29:106
A square rod, one end forming a close loop, the other end bent to a tapering curve this end is incomplete and much damaged by rust.
9.3 × 0.9 × 0.8 cm, loop diameter 2.1 cm.

Three iron nails   Pl. 23 107–109
The nail heads are either flat or slightly domed. Only one nail is complete.
Length 9 7 cm, 4.7 cm and 2.5 cm.

Box-shaped mount of iron   Pl. 27·112
Perhaps a ferrule for a handle of circular section, it is

made in one piece, of cylindrical shape with a thick base. The upper edge is damaged and incomplete. The original height was probably irregular There are traces of a deposit on the inside perhaps of wood without actual fibres.

Maximum height 3.7 cm, diameter at top 3.1 cm, diameter at bottom 2.9· thickness of base about 0.7 cm.

Mount of sheet-iron   Pl. 19:113
Mount with three rivet-holes which have raised edges at the back.
13.5 × 2.7–1 7 × 0.2–0.1 cm.

Angular mount of sheet-iron   Pl. 19:114
The mount retains a pin (length 1.0 cm, with no traces of wood) and is pierced by two holes from pins or rivets.
4.2 × 4.0; width of arms 1.8–1.6 cm, thickness 0.05 cm.

Iron loop   Pl. 19:115
The loop may be part of a handle attachment or hinge cf the hinges on the chest, no. 132) It is made from an iron rod of circular section with the ends hammered to a thin plate of irregular rectangular shape. There are two irregular rivet-holes near the loop and at the other end of the plate there is an asymmetrical rhomboid hole which may have been caused by damage.
7.0 × 3.0 × 0.6–0.1 cm.

Part of a band-shaped mount of sheet-iron   Pl. 19:116
The mount has three irregularly spaced holes one a circular rivet-hole, the other two angular The sides may be original, one end is cut and the other damaged.
4.8 × 1.8 × 0.2 cm.

Square plate of (?)sheet-copper   Pl. 19:117
In antiquity the plate probably had a large rivet-hole at each corner one corner is missing) The raised edges around the holes on the back presumably indicate that the plate was originally attached to a soft material such as wood or leather On the front faint rings 0.6 cm in diameter left by the rivet-heads can be traced round the holes.
3 1 × 3.0 × 0.1 cm.

Iron loop   Pl. 29:118
Loop made from a round iron rod terminating in a straight tapering shank by which the loop was riveted to a (?)wooden object 4.0–4.5 cm thick. No wood fibres remain.
10.5 × 3.5 × 0.7 cm, washer 2.2 × 1.8 × 0.1 cm.

(?)Part of a handle attachment of iron   Pl. 25.119
Round rod bent at one end to form a loop and hammered to the forged plate which is broken off the break cutting across a large rivet-hole cf. no 125 c which looks similar and has the same patina, however the two pieces do not fit)
3.6 × 2.2 × 0.6–0.1 cm.

Coarse round iron rod   Pl. 30:120
The rod is cut off at each end, and its surface is somewhat rough.
7.9 × 1 7 cm.

Part of iron band of uniform width   Pl. 25·121
The band is slightly curved, both edges are original and one is slightly thickened with a narrow flange on the inside.
4.7 × 1 9 × 0.3 cm.

Part of a broad iron band   Pl. 22:124
(?)Stamping pad. In the centre the object has two narrow rectangular depressions, one of which has an uneven bottom. It is broken at both ends.
6.4 × 2.5 × 0.5–0.7 cm.

Miscellaneous fragments

Sixty-six 'fragments are listed under no. 125 in the museum s catalogue:

Pls. 24, 25 29 and 30:125

a (?) Blank. a fragment like a small spearhead with a central ridge on each side. One end is lightly hammered to resemble a tang, and the other end is cut. There are no cutting edges (Pl. 30)
10.7 × 2.8 ×1.0–0.6 cm.

b Part of a raw iron bar one end is roughly shaped as a tang of circular section and cut irregularly at the end. The other end is also cut, but rounded, and has a notch in the edge (Pl. 25)
8.9 × 2.4 ×1 1 cm.

c Incomplete (?) knife-blade the back and the unsharpened edge diverge slightly· both ends are cut.

Note. It is possible that this object is part of the (?)handle attachment no. 119.

d) Part of a (?)trefoil stand. a portion of a flat leg with a tapering foot set at right angles. Both ends are cut, cf. nos. 92, 93 (Pl. 29).
7.2 × 2.4–0.7 × 0.4 cm.

e–m Nine small pieces of iron from indeterminate objects the objects are mostly of sheet-iron, several have rivet-holes or rivet-heads attached, the pieces vary widely in size and shape. A very thin curved iron rod 125 m) of rectangular section retains a pin with a small head near the centre. This fragment measures 6.5 × 0.5 × 0.1 cm (Pl. 30)

n) Six small pieces of round or square rods with traces of working. One round rod has been damaged by bending. A fragment of a round faceted rod may be part of the hook of a handle. This fragment measures 2.6 × 0.7 × 0.6 cm (Pl. 25).
Lengths 6.2–2.8 cm.

o Three pieces of sheet-iron. much damaged by rust and bending. The smallest piece is pierced by a fairly large rivet hole.
Largest piece 13.5 × 13.0 × 0.1 cm. (Pl. 25)

p) Eight curved thin narrow iron rods two of the pieces represent about half a ring, a third piece about two thirds of a ring. Sizes and widths vary (Pl. 30)
Largest piece 4.3 × 1.0 × 0.2 cm; smallest piece 2.5 × 0.4 × 0.1 cm.

r) Six pieces of scrap. some are probably parts of raw-iron bars. Dimensions vary· both ends are cut on all pieces except in one case where one rounded end is preserved.
Largest piece 3.6 × 2.7 × 1.0 cm; smallest piece 2.7 × 0.8 × 0.4 cm.

s Fifteen pieces of sheet-iron of varying sizes shapes and dimensions. All are indeterminate and badly rusted, some are bent.
Largest piece 4.9 × 3.5 × 0.4 cm; smallest piece 1 7 × 1.0 × 0.1 cm.

t) Half an iron collar(?) for a heavy handle: the smooth original surface of the upper edge is preserved, one end is straight and even and may be original. The remaining edges are very uneven and badly damaged. The piece has been damaged by bending.
Diameter about 3.9 cm, height 2.5 cm, thickness 0.2 cm.

u) Folded and hammered iron plate originally probably circular with rivet-holes near the edge. The distance between the holes is about 4.5 cm. There is possibly a slightly domed rivet-head (Pl. 24)
Diameter about 17 cm, thickness 0.2 cm.

Fifteen objects of iron   Pls. 25 and 30:126
In the museum's catalogue these objects are listed under no. 126:

a Eleven pieces of raw-iron bars of rectangular section and varying dimensions. All are cut at both ends, (Pls. 25 and 30).
Lengths from 2.5 cm to 10.0 cm.

b Two pieces of an iron bar probably with one original rounded end, the other end is cut.
4.8 × 2.5 × 0.3–0.6 cm and 9.0 × 1 9 × 1.2 cm.

c Piece of an iron rod with partly grooved sides. The surface is very rough, and the rod tapers. It is damaged or perhaps cut at both ends (Pl. 25).
8.4 × 1.5 × 0.2–0.6 cm.

d) Lump of iron consisting of seven pieces of rawiron bars like those described above, lightly forged together The individual pieces are of varying dimensions (Pl. 30).
Maximum measurements of a piece 13.8 × 4.3 × 0.8 cm, total weight 1291 g.

Brass cake   Pl. 27·127
The cake is irregular in shape: one side is very rough and pitted, the other is flat with slight irregular ridges, reflecting the texture of the surface on which the metal was poured.
5.5 × 3 7 × 0.7 cm.

Tine of elk antler   Pl. 23 128
Sawn-off end of an elk-antler tine.
6.0 × 3.3 × 1 7 cm.

Two pieces of maple wood   Pl. 28.129–130
The pieces have oval sections, are well finished and cut at both ends. They are not otherwise shaped and there is no indication of their use. The present condition of the wood is hard and firm, and the light colour has been preserved.
No. 129: 8.0 × 2.0 × 2.8 cm.
No. 130: 8.5 × 2.0 × 2.9 cm.
No. 131 the catalogue lists another wood fragment under this number but this is now missing.

Part of a twisted rope of leather strands   Pl. 29:133
The rope is Z-twisted from three S-twisted strands. It is very fragile.
The largest piece: length about 5.0 cm, thickness 1.0 cm.

Notes on nos. 129–131 133 and the unnumbered cauldron fragment (p. 11).
There is no information on where the pieces of wood and the rope fragments were found. It is possible that they were in the chest, as they are not included in the descriptions compiled before conservation and thus before the chest was completely emptied of all the smallest fragments.
It is possible that the cauldron fragment (unnumbered, p. 11) was found in the same way This object was not included in the preliminary descriptions of the find, nor is it in the museum's present catalogue.

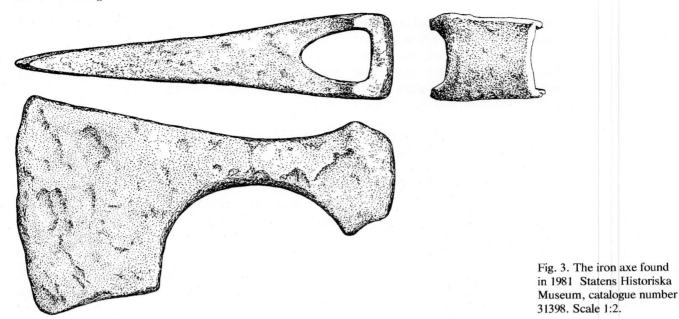

Fig. 3. The iron axe found in 1981 Statens Historiska Museum, catalogue number 31398. Scale 1:2.

A find from Mästermyr in 1981

Axe of iron   SHM 31398: Fig. 3
A broad-edged axe with marked flanges at the hafthole.
The butt is rectangular and slightly convex.
20.0 × 12.0 × 4.7 cm.

This is probably a tool axe. Its type does not correspond to any of the axes found in the tool chest. Petersen 1919) records several examples of this type Rygh 555 (Rygh 1885) but refers them to weapon axes. he does not include this type among tool axes 1951) The circumstances of this find are related in chapter 1

3. Pre-medieval comparative material
by Greta Arwidsson

All the tools in the Mästermyr find seem to be of types which may have been used in Scandinavia since the early Iron Age. The most important aspect of the find is that it consists of a comprehensive collection of tools associated with both smithing and carpentry While other Swedish tool finds consist of small selections of tools, such as would have been used by someone engaged in light smithing, carpentry and general repair work, we have here probably an almost complete range of tools to fit the needs both of a blacksmith and a carpenter Although this is a closed find, we cannot necessarily conclude that smithing and carpentry were at this time practised by the same person. There is considerable evidence to confirm the high social status of the professional blacksmith from the early Iron Age to more recent times (cf Gösta Berg, *The Smith*)

Roman gravestones sometimes honour the memory of craftsmen of different kinds, and smiths graves featured tools associated with Vulcan, the god of the smith's art: sledge hammers, hammers and often also tongs and anvils (for example the gravestone from Sens, showing the smith and his tools in relief Smith 1861, pp. V 167 and pl. XIX). The same tools are seen in representations from the Merovingian period, the Viking Age and the medieval period (Hauck 1977 Müller-Wille 1977 fig. 1–2 and Lindqvist 1941 p. 194) Swedish examples include the representation of Völund's smithy with two sledge hammers and two tongs on the picture-stone from Ardre, Gotland (Lindqvist 1941 pl. 59) and the more complete equipment of sledge hammer tong, anvil and bellows portrayed on the rune rock at Ramsund, Södermanland (Lindqvist 1914, Brate & Wessén 1924–1936, Sö 101)

The carpenter and his tools are also sometimes portrayed. A frequently quoted example of carpenters and boat-builders at work is a scene on the Bayeux tapestry (Stenton 1957 fig. 38–39 pl. VII). However there are also Roman examples, including a magnificent gold-glass bowl with a representation of a Roman nobleman surrounded by six craftsmen working with saw broad axe, (?)auger chisel, hammer and (?)plane, and also building a boat (Schubert & von Hoerschelman 1978, no. 43 and Kisa 1908, p. 867 fig. 357). The bowl can probably be dated to the latter half of the fourth century

A gravestone from Ravenna shows a carpenter at work on a boat with a broad axe (Gaitzsch and Mattäus 1980, pl. 24, cf. several examples of carpenters gravestones in this work)

There is a wide range of material relevant to a study of when the different tool types were introduced in Scandinavia, and where they came from. It is clear that the types did not develop in Scandinavia, but were already distinctly specialised when they were introduced. For our purpose the study of Continental material may be restricted to the Iron Age.

Iron was used along with bronze as early as the Hallstatt period. However in Central Europe it was the Celts of the La Tène period who developed iron technology which was to reach its height in the early Iron Age. Traces of mining and smelting furnaces as well as the large quantities of iron bars demonstrate that iron was in good supply Tools and weapon types bear witness to the standardisation of production which resulted in the spread of highly-developed skills within the extensive Celtic empire in central and eastern Europe (cf e.g. Déchelette 1914, II Vouga 1923) The weapons of the Celts are usually known from grave finds and hoards (Déchelette 1914, II, 3 pp. 1106f· Filip 1956, fig. 84 and Vouga 1923) while their heavier tools are usually found in the settlement deposits and debris from the fortified towns (*oppida* from which their social organisation derived. From Bibracte and Vix in France (Dehn 1976, Joffroy 1960) Manching in South Germany (Jacobi 1974) Sarmizegetusa in Rumania (Miclea 1980) Lozna, Botosania in Rumania (Silvia 1980) and many similar sites and hoards, sets of tools are found, whose forms and types all continue to be used in Europe throughout the Iron Age and up to the medieval period and the present day

A particularly interesting find from Hungary was published as early as 1906 by Darnay Kálmán in *Archaeologiai Értesitö* XXVI with several illustrations) The site is in Szalacska within Nagyberk in the Somogy district of south-west Hungary In the remains of an *oppidum* a burnt-down minting and metal-casting workshop was excavated, complete with the whole equipment of several types of anvils tongs hammers, chisels augers knives and moulds. Celtic coins together with their dies found in the deposit provide an approximate date in the latter half of the last century B.C.[1]

The large bog find from La Tène by the Neuchâtel Lake in Switzerland, which gives its name to the period, is important for a comparative study of weapon and tool types, although the finds is no longer regarded as chronologically uniform (Vouga 1923 Schwab 1972)

However some grave finds provide examples of both weapons and important tool types, allowing comparative and chronological conclusions to be drawn.

The contents of a large burial mound with a cremation deposit from Celles, Auvergne, France (Pagés-Allary 1903 p. 385) included the following objects, much damaged by fire: a lance head, two shield-bosses, three larger knives, two saw-blades, two coarse files, a band-iron, two chisels three leather knives, nine awls two hammers and a sickle. The find is dated to La Tène III on the basis of the weapon types and of the pottery which belongs to at least five types. However the tools in the Celles burial are mainly smaller types used for woodwork.

Roman tool finds come mainly from occupation deposits in towns and forts. W Gaitzsch (1980) has recently published a compilation of Roman tool types used for working with metal, wood and stone. Some of his most important groups of finds are from the ruins of Ostia and Pompei, from the town of Aquileia and from Niederbieber in the Rhineland, with its remains of *castellum* and *vicus* A section of his Summary (p. 256) is worth quoting in full.

The rich and varied spectrum of Roman tools exerted an influence on the development of tools up to the onset of the machine age. Between the Roman and Modern Age new tools did not come into existence. Nearly all forms were either already fully developed or appear for the first time in Roman archaeological contexts.

Gaitzsch's list of *Hort- und Sammelfunde eiserner und Römischer Werkzeuge und Geräte* (1980) includes many finds of wood-working and agricultural tools. However two very large closed finds of smiths tools are also included. one from Kreimbach, Heidenburg, Rhenish Bavaria, comprising a hundred objects and another from München-Grünwald, found in a Roman (?)fort, which included tools and several mounts to a total of more than a hundred objects. It is likely that the tools were stored in a wooden chest (Lindenschmidt 1911 vol. V pl. 46).

As the Scandinavians had close contacts with the cultures of central and western Europe both in the Celtic and the Roman Iron Age, it is remarkable that only in the late Roman Iron Age do the standardised

tool types of Europe become more widely represented in Scandinavian finds Various reasons may be suggested for this. One possibility is that heavier iron tools were not produced from high-quality iron and that badly rusted objects have passed unnoticed during unsystematic digging. It is not altogether surprising that the earliest find of a heavier tool axe—a socketed axe—was made in a Danish votive deposit. This was at Brå near Horsens in Jutland, the axe was in poor condition and lay at the bottom of a large cauldron of bronze and iron (Klindt-Jensen 1953) However Klindt-Jensen considered that both the axe and the cauldron had been imported from Celtic Europe.

Another important reason may be related to burial customs in Scandinavia during the earlier Iron Age. The inhumation or cremation burials contains weapons and dress accessories but few objects which can be described as tools, usually only a single knife is present, although combinations such as a sickle and an awl or a leather knife and an awl also occur (Nylén 1955 Sahlström 1954, Sahlström & Gejvall 1948; Ekholm 1944, fig. 24; Hagberg 1967 II pp. 115· Brøndsted III, 1966, pp. 160, 163) Occasionally tongs (or perhaps shears) occur as early as the third period (B.C.) of the Iron Age, while small tongs and shears of the type used for shearing sheep become more common in the burials of the early Roman Iron Age (Nylén 1955 fig. 110, tongs or shears and a large knife from Änge in Alva, Gotland, Ekholm 1939, p. 18, Klindt-Jensen 1978 e.g. the weapon graves no. 334, fig. 62, no. 825, fig. 88 no. 969, fig. 118, and no. 1072, fig. 34, Stenberger 1935 tongs and hammer alone) The presence of scissors in weapon graves, in combination with a certain type of razor—with a semi-circular edge—suggests that these were probably a toilet accessory closely modelled on Roman prototypes cf. Ekholm 1939; however the identification of the razor is here in question)

In the later Roman Iron Age (*c.* 200–400 A.D.) there are graves with hammers tongs and anvils which have led several scholars to identify them as smiths and goldsmiths graves (Brøndsted 1960, fig. 133 distribution map and 234 with fig. 224; Stenberger 1935 cf Brøndsted III, 1966, p. 250 and Werner 1954)

Blacksmiths and carpenters' tools are first represented in the Danish bog finds, where they are particularly plentiful in the find from Vimose on Fyn dated to *c* 100–300 A.D. (Engelhardt 1869). Large quentities of weapons accompanied the tools and various household goods. Among the heavier tools were about twenty axes, three adzes, four hammers, two tongs an anvil, a rasp, a file, two draw-knives, two planes, three socketed chisels, two socketed gouges, a spoon-auger a three-pronged tool and a collection of about one

---

Tamás Sárkány Stockholm, has kindly translated the text from the Hungarian.

hundred rivets. There is also an example of a finely-shaped carved plane.

Some Swedish bog finds from the same period also contain similar smiths tools. As in the Danish bog finds, weapons, horse-trappings and tools are found together at Skedemosse on Öland (Hagberg 1967 I–II) and a small (?)hoard from Rommelsjö, Öggestorp, Småland, consists of a sledge hammer two hammers, smithing tongs and a file together with a spear-head of a type which is usually dated to the fourth or fifth centuries A.D. (Arbman 1963 p. 77 fig. 41).

Farm complexes and large single houses from throughout the earlier Scandinavian Iron Age are now known, and many of them have been systematically excavated. The lack of tools and of larger iron objects in general is perhaps remarkable, particularly where there is evidence that a house was lived in when it burned down. A possible explanation is that the owner would have searched through the debris for iron objects that might be re-used. (Brøndsted 1960, III, Beskow-Sjöberg 1977· Stenberger 1933 1935 1955 Klindt-Jensen 1957 and Hvass 1979.)

Equally few iron tools are mostly found in the settlement sites of the late Iron Age, (cf. Bender-Jørgensen & Skov 1980, p. 132, Hvass 1980, p. 169 and Stoumann 1980, p. 115), but heavier tools occur with increasing frequency in the grave finds of the Vendel period and Viking Age.

Grieg's paper on *Smedeverktøj i norske graver* (Smiths tools in Norwegian graves) 1922 and Petersen s compendious work on *Vikingetidens redskaper* (The tools of the Viking Age) 1951 demonstrate that men s graves containing smiths tools became common in the eighth century (the Vendel period) and that at the same time carpenters and wood-carvers tools also became particularly numerous.[2]

Jan Petersen attempted to define smith's grave' thus. a find where, other than weapons and driving or riding equipment, the only tools are smithing tools, and particularly where these are the most numerous This can be seen as an acceptable definition, but as Wallander has pointed out (1979, p. 8) Petersen himself did not always abide by it. He apparently wished to categorise as smiths graves finds where only one or two smithing tools were found along with weapons and bridles (1951 114). Wallander has suggested that only one or two smithing tools in a grave may be regarded as symbolic grave gifts, i.e. *pars pro toto* gifts (1979, p. 48).

While finding Petersen s attempt at a definition

acceptable, I consider that the appraisal of individual examples must be very subjective. We know of many richly-furnished men s burials which contain objects associated with daily life, as well as food-stuffs of various kinds. Obvious examples are the boat burials which seem to have been equipped as for a long journey as they would have been when the men were alive cf. Arwidsson 1954, p. 16).

However a good example of a smith s grave is presumably the primary burial in a damaged mound from Ytre Elgsnes, Trondenes Södra Troms, Norway (Simonsen 1953 Sjøvold 1974, pp. 138, 307) Above the skull of a man were found the remains of iron mounts from a wooden chest which contained 'a large pair of tongs, a hammer two files, a punch and a forge-stone' as well as two knives, a spoon-auger and a socketed axe. Thus these are mainly true blacksmiths tools, the spoon-auger may be seen as a carpenter's tool—unless this tool, along with the knives and the axe, is to be regarded as an example of the smith s work. This is the interpretation many scholars have given to the large Norwegian grave find from Bygland, Brunteberg, Morgedal, Kviteseid, Telemark. Of the one hundred and twenty objects in this find, only just over 12 % were weapons (four swords, four spear-heads and seven weapon axes) while 25 % were smithing tools including four sledge hammers, two coarse tongs, a plate-shear two hammers an anvil, a draw-plate and a file, along with several minor tools and pieces of raw iron (Blindheim 1962) Charlotte Blindheim sees this find, which came from a cremation burial, as the equipment of a man who practised both blacksmithing and fine smithing, because she regards the silver-decorated weapons in the find as examples of his work.

The theory that the smith occupied a high social position is supported by some Norwegian grave finds from the Viking Age containing both weapons and smithing tools such as the grave from Risöy Hadsel, Lofoten-Vesterålen (Nicolaissen 1924, p. 31 and Sjøvold 1974, pp. 111 308) and that from Skredtveit, Mo, Telemark (Grieg 1938–40, inv no. 26637)

The boat grave from Ile de Groix, Brittany may perhaps be compared with the Bygland find in Telemark. It contained weapons a sword, spear-head, arrowheads shields (twenty-one shield-bosses) and a weapon axe as well as an apparently quite extensive set of tools (Arbman & Nilsson 1969 Müller-Wille 1977) Most of the objects were badly damaged on the pyre and are fragmentary It is also likely that the material from the burial is incomplete. The tools, which do not now include any heavier implements, seem in this case to be part of the equipment taken on a long journey—a chest of tools for repairs and minor work.

---

[2] See also, for instance, Wallander 1979, tables 50–51

An example of what are thought to be goldsmiths graves is that from Gannor Lau, Gotland (Stenberger 1935)

The rich Norwegian grave from Vestly Time, Rogaland (Müller-Wille 1977 p. 167 cf Wallander 979 p. 202) is another probable early smith s grave. The set of tools, which was apparently contained in a small chest, was obviously intended for fine smithing as they were all small and slight. As there is a comprehensive collection of weapons, household utensils and other grave goods, it would seem that, in this case at least, the tool chest cannot be seen as suggesting the dead man s profession, any more than the weapons can. The Vestly grave belongs to the Migration period and is comparable to a large number of weapon graves with complete equipments of this kind (Shetelig 1912A and in particular 1912B Sjøvold 1962). However men s graves with a full complement of weapons rarely contain tool chests as well. At this time chests of this sort seem to have appeared mainly in women s graves, holding the small tools specifically used by women.

A recently-discovered cremation grave of the Vendel period from Drocksjön/Angersjö, Hälsingland, can apparently be correctly described as the grave of a fine smith because it contained a complete equipment and all of the small tools were elegantly finished (Preliminary publication in *Historiska Nyheter* Statens Historiska Museer 1982, p. 6).

However there are no known tools from the Viking Age used exclusively for fine smithing found in combination with weapons.

*

Many research institutes in Sweden and elsewhere are at present studying iron technology and several projects have already produced significant results. Among these are *Excavations at Helgö* vol. V 1 (1978) and Pleiner 1962 and 1975 In its Research Series H, the History of Mining committee of Jernkontoret has also published no. 9 Serning 1973 and no. 17 Magnusson 1978.

A comprehensive technical and metallographic analysis of the entire Mästermyr find would be desirable from many points of view However pending the results of some of the projects mentioned above, no such studies are currently under way Only a few analysis reports are appended to this work (Appendix II), these were commissioned by Gösta Berg and carried out by S. Modin at the Metallographic Institute in Stockholm in 1953

The skills of the Viking Age smith

In the catalogue every identifiable tool has been described by the common name applied to such tools up to the present day In his contribution to this study Gösta Berg describes comparable types in ethnological collections and in archives relating to old crafts. These form the basis for the terms used in the catalogue and also provide information on how these tools were used and the crafts to which they belong.

In addition I believe it would be of interest to examine the smithing skills to which the material from Mästermyr bears witness.

The small number of metallographic analyses carried out on these tools (Appendix II) demonstrate that the adze (no. 63) the axe (no. 62) and the spoon-auger (no. 50) had all been given steeled cutting edges by *forge welding* edges of carbon-rich steel were welded to the softer carbon-poor iron of the tools themselves thus improving their performance.

Welding was also used to close the links in the heavy chain (no. 17) and in the trace-rings (nos 89–90) However the most common method of joining was apparently *riveting* as seen on most of the objects on pls 16–17 (the steelyard no. 1 the fire-grid no. 31 and the bells nos. 26–28) on the tongs nos. 43–44 and the hack-saw no. 36. The fragment of a fairly large iron cauldron (pl. 25 unnumbered) exemplifies the method, common in the later Scandinavian Iron Age, of producing cooking vessels by riveting together a large number of iron plates. There are Vendel Period examples from Vendel and Valsgärde (Stolpe and Arne 1912, Arwidsson 1954 and 1977) and many such vessels occur in Norwegian graves of the Viking Age (Petersen 1951 p. 369)

The copper-alloy cauldrons nos. 19 and 23 (pl. 24) were repaired by riveting on copper alloy patches but the sheets which make up the cauldrons were originally joined by *overlapping and stitching'* a technique used until quite recently in the manufacture of copper vessels. For this technique, see comprehensive studies by Oldeberg 1966) and Trotzig 1978) with a critical appraisal of Oldeberg.

The iron plates of the padlocks (nos. 10–12) are joined by *soldering* and the yellow solder (probably brass) can clearly be seen on nos. 10 and 11 Whether or not there are traces of brass plating cannot be ascertained cf. Gösta Berg's comments on the bells)

Plating the application of a thin coating of metal alloy (copper or perhaps brass) occurs on the bells (nos. 26–28)

Beating and chasing must have been employed in the production of plates and sheets of both iron and copper or bronze. Thicker rods would have been hammered.

Stamp punches of various kinds were used to produce the few ornaments which occur on the Mästermyr objects. The bronze details on the steelyard (no. 1) are decorated with ring-and-dot motifs and punched straight or beaded lines The iron surfaces of the weight, ring and hook are decorated with groups of punched triangles

The use of punched ornaments is also seen on the stamping pad (no. 85) with its many punched impressions and the fragmentary punch (no. 84) cf the discussion of these ornaments in chapter 5 below)

Twisted rods are used for decoration on the padlocks (nos. 10–12) the steelyard (no. 1) and the key (no. 2) The twisted shanks of the trace-rings (nos 87–88) may have been due to the method of construction rather than any desire for decoration.

The chest and some of the tools found within it. Photographic arrangement by Iwar Andersson.

4. Some ethnological aspects of the find
by Gösta Berg

The chest

The storage of tools in chests, rather than in barrels or sacks, dates far back into antiquity A Bronze Age tool-chest, thought to have belonged to an itinerant smith, was found in Pomerania (Singer 1954 p. 576). Iron mounts are sometimes found together with tools from the Viking Age, indicating that the tools were kept in a chest. This was the case, for instance, in the large and valuable find in Bø, Gloppen, Sogn og Fjordane, Norway (*Bergens Museums årbog* 1913 pp. 24ff.) The chests themselves have of course only been preserved in lake and bog finds. A chest with carpenters and smiths tools from about the time of the birth of Christ was recovered from the water at Waltham Abbey Essex, England (Manning 1978). Of particular interest in connection with the find from Mästermyr is the chest, with Celtic ornament and containing tools of different kinds, which was found in a bog on Birsay Orkney in 1885 (Cursiter 1886, pp. 47ff.). Stephen Cruden dates it to *c.*800 and adds that it was 'probably dropped by one of the inmates flying before the Norse pirates who Dicuil, writing *c* 820, reports as having recently caused the flight of monks from the Faeroes (Cruden 1965 p. 25).

It is most probable, however that the chest from Mästermyr was not originally intended as a tool-chest but that this was a secondary use. Several factors point to this. there are no handles or other means by which the chest could be transported, the construction is light; and the lock suggests a storage place for lighter more fragile and valuable articles than heavy tools. Chests were the most common and versatile method of storage during the medieval period and it can be taken for granted that their use went back to prehistory (Anker and Topelius 1963).

The chest is made of oak and the sides are butted to the ends and secured with pegs. However the bottom plank is not only morticed and tenoned to the ends but also set into rabbets in the ends and sides.

The chest can best be compared to the three chests in the Oseberg find. Like these, the sides and ends slope inwards towards the top to increase stability There are no mounts other than the hinges and the lock-plate and the construction is therefore generally rather weak. A couple of centuries later this type of chest was replaced by one with corner posts into which the side planks were slotted.[1] This type achieved great popularity and was the most common until the introduction of dovetailed furniture in the sixteenth century Chests of similar construction to the Mästermyr example also occur later The remarkable church chests from Voxtorp, Rydaholm, and Ryssby in Småland are made by this method. They date from the end of the twelfth century and around 1200 (Karlson 1928 p. 58 cf. Engelstad 1944 and von Schoultz 1949 and quoted literature) With half-lap joints at the corners and along the sides and bottom, this early construction continued for a long time in folk art. However these chests were usually fitted with more elaborate iron mounts (Homman 1941) Greta Arwidsson has rightly pointed out the difficulties involved in reconstructing chests from the mounts preserved in archaeological finds (Arwidsson 1942 pp. 78ff. on such attempts cf. Kaland 1969 pp. 129ff.) [2]

The locks

The lock (nos. 13–15) on the chest from Mästermyr is relatively well preserved, and therefore contributes to a better understanding of the construction of this type of lock. Our knowledge has hitherto been based on similar examples from Birka and Vendel, but these are in a very poor state of preservation and the conclusions drawn from them in historical expositions on this subject have frequently been very misleading e.g. Erixon 1946, whereas cf. Hellner 1948 pp. 156, 176f.)

It is of draw-lock type and examples of very similar doorlocks were found in remote areas of Dalarna even as late as the nineteenth century The lock works on the

---

[1] A chest of this type, which can be dated by its ornament to the first half of the twelfth century has recently been acquired by Oldsaksamlingen in Oslo (*Universitetets Olsaksamlings tillvækst* 1973–6, 1979, pp. 21 f.).

[2] The smith Lars Samuel Lyander of Lau (born 1821) had a tool-chest with mounts and a canted lid, which was carefully measured by Mathias Klintberg. It was known as a *verkfat* (Klintberg, notes *Anteckningar*).

principle that a key with a two- or three-toothed bit lifts a spring with corresponding holes the bolt is thus released and can be pulled back, either by using the key itself, as on the chest, or as in the case of doorlocks, by a draw-ring on the outside of the door Neither key from Mästermyr (nos 2–3) fits the lock of the chest, but these keys belonged to locks of the same type, presumably fitted to chests or boxes of similar construction. The use of this type of lock for such purposes ceased around the end of the medieval period and the beginning of the sixteenth century when it was replaced by the tumbler lock which dominated the development of locks up until the present day

The three smaller locks (nos. 10–12) are padlocks, also designed to secure boxes and other containers. In their use and construction these padlocks are in every respect equivalent to the bolt locks which were introduced towards the end of the medieval period and completely replaced the earlier type found at Mästermyr (Berg, Christensen jr and Liestøl, 1966; Homman, 1966; cf also Blomqvist 1940) The keys of the earlier type are spade-shaped with perforations which engage the wards of the lock and release the spring. No such keys are included in the find, but they are very thin and flimsy and are easily lost.

The catalogue of a temporary exhibition in the State Historical Museum relates that smiths in Lima parish, Dalarna, sometimes sold the locks they made by weight (this information is probably taken from the late Olle Homman, *Fynd och fältarbeten* 1937 p. 31) It has unfortunately not been possible to confirm this statement.

Holger Arbman suggests that the presence in the find of loose lock-plates and springs (nos. 4–8) indicates that the smith himself made locks This must remain an open question (Arbman 1937). Traces of brass on one of the padlocks suggest that it may have been brass-plated (*brassat*) Smiths in Lima, Dalarna, still treated padlocks in this manner in the nineteenth century (*Lima och Transtrand* 1982 p. 342ff for brass-plating, see p. 28 below)

The chain

According to the reports, the long forged chain (no. 17) was wound round the chest when it was found. The ring which is still attached at one end indicates that this was probably a tether presumably for a horse. Horse tethers were usually about eight or nine metres long, and therefore only about a third of the original chain remains. The other end would have had a fetter-lock which was fastened round the hind leg of the horse. There may have been a swivel attached somewhere

along the chain. A comparison may be made with the dog leashes found in graves at Vendel and Valsgärde (Petersen 1951 pp. 416 f Arwidsson 1942 pl. 29) The length of the chain, 2.4 m, argues against its being intended for suspending cooking vessels even though a pot chain in the Oseberg find was about 2 m long. Nor is it likely that it was used on a boat, as the Scandinavian medieval literary sources only mention the use of hemp and walrus hide as mooring ropes and anchor hawsers (Falk 1912 p. 80)

The manufacture of such chains was a fairly complicated process. The individual links were forged on round mandrels of the appropriate size. When they had been welded together they were given a half-turn twist to render the tether more flexible and prevent tangles This was done by inserting two rods at each end of the link and twisting in opposite directions. The chain was made in short sections which were then joined together (*Lima och Transtrand* 1982 p. 342)

The fire-grid

The fire-grid (no. 31) which was intended to hang from the ceiling in a work-place with an earth floor was found throughout Europe. Mathias Klintberg noted an example in a smithy in Lau Gotland, of which he made an inventory early this century It was used as a source of light when night forging took place, with tarred firewood or a lamp In this case the fire-grid consisted of an iron plate suspended by an iron chain 150 cm from the ceiling.[3] A similar device for lighting a threshing barn from Gräsmark, Värmland, is in the collection of the Nordiska Museet (Ambrosiani 1913) Another is known from Ulrika, Östergötland (Carlsson 1958 p. 124)

In these examples resinous sticks were used as firewood, and it is obvious that ash would collect on the plate and reduce the effectiveness of the light. Wilhelm Bomann observed how this was avoided in Lower Saxony (north of Celle) by placing a couple of fire-dogs on top of the plate (Bomann 1929 pp. 112f.)

However the fire-grid from Mästermyr where the burnt-out material is allowed to fall to the floor has parallels elsewhere. I have noted an example in the Musée de la vie Wallone, Liège, but the type seems to have been particularly common in south-west Europe (Robillard 1965 p. 45 Chartres France, Krüger 1939 p.

---

[3] The reference in Klintberg and Gustavsson (1972–, p. 61 illustrations, part 6) is misleading. This illustration shows an iron tool used in leister-fishing. Klintberg made two sketches of the hanging fire-grid in the smithy

185 on the distribution in Spain, cf. also Alvar 1978 p. 176 and Violant i Simorra 1948 p 176) [4]

Fire-irons of grid type are also common in Eastern Europe. Dimitri Zelenin illustrates one example from the Minsk district in white Russia (1972 p. 28) and there are also examples from the Ukraine (*Sovjetskaja Etnografija* 1953 Bruckner 1939 p. 159) [5] from Poland and Czechoslovakia (Moszyński 1929 pp. 587f. and quoted literature). They even occur in Albania (*Etnografia Shqiptare* 1 p. 128). The method of suspension varies—in Russia two chains are used—but most correspond closely to the Mästermyr type.

It is clear that fire-grids of this type have a wide distribution in Europe and that they were also used in work-places other than smithies. However the grid type required an earth or stone floor This device must have been of great use to the itinerant craftsman.

The bells

The three bells (nos. 26–28) are the earliest known of their kind in Scandinavia. They are made from a folded sheet of metal and are very similar in construction to more recent cow-bells. Nils Lithberg has studied a large number of these and has distinguished three main types, of which the Mästermyr bells most closely resemble type B (Lithberg 1914 an attempt by Nilsson (1941 p. 32) to establish a geographical distribution of these types was unsuccessful). The type is also known on Gotland in later material. The method of manufacture is well-known through many descriptions including Matsson 1953 cf. *Lima och Transtrand* 1982, pp. 342 ff.). The raw material was iron blanks which were hammered into fairly thin sheets.

The joints in the bells had to be made tight in order to improve their resonance: in forged bells this was achieved by plating the inside and outside with a thin layer of copper or brass. This was known as to *brassa* the bell. The process is based on the fact that iron and copper fuse in high temperatures, it could be done even without adding a special fusing flux. The copper plating, which also occurs in other contexts such as on padlocks, further served to protect against rust. The bells from Mästermyr were copper-plated, although the plating is now very much worn away The *brassning* was achieved by placing a piece of charcoal inside the

bell and covering the bell inside and out with copper strips. It was then covered in clay to which horse dung or the like had been added to make it more porous. The clay lump was placed in the hearth and great heat produced with the aid of bellows The clay had to be turned over from time to time to achieve a smooth surface and this process continued even after it had been taken out to cool.

The bells are also unique in Scandinavia, as they have two clappers In this respect they are similar to wooden bells found in many areas in more recent times Lithberg illustrates a wooden bell with two clappers from Garda, Gotland (in Gotlands Fornsal, Visby) Another example, carved in oak, was found in a bog on the borders between Halland and Västergötland (now in the Varberg Museum) It is possible that this can be dated to the Roman Iron Age by pollen analysis (Sandklef 1951). A very similar bell from a bog-find in Borås Museum, Västergötland, is mentioned by Sandklef. In both cases only one clapper remains but there are suspension holes for two. A bell carved of oak from a Jutland bog-find is of similar type, although all three clappers are missing (now in Ålborg Historical Museum, Neubert 1969 pp. 59f.) In other parts of Sweden wooden bells with one clapper are common, but they seem to be modelled on iron bells. Bells with two or three clappers appear to be found mainly in eastern Europe. They are common in Estonia, Latvia and Lithuania, East Prussia, south-west Poland and the Ukraine, and also occur in the Caucasus with a somewhat different suspension arrangement, as well as outside Europe (Manninen 1933 pp. 152ff.)

The two clappers in the Mästermyr bells are indeed a very curious feature and may suggest the existence of two different cultural spheres in which bells of different types occur However our limited knowledge of the conditions in the East does not allow any definite conclusions in this matter It is clear however, that the bells of folded sheet-iron are closely related to the bells which appear in the British Isles at a period which corresponds to the Viking Age and early medieval period in Sweden (Anderson 1881 pp. 167–215 Bourke 1980) These bells were used to call people to worship and also for ecclesiastical processions of various kinds. Some of these bells, which pre-date the cast bronze bells, closely resemble the Mästermyr bells in construction and size.

The bells differ from common cow-bells by their considerable size: not less than 25 cm in length they must also have been very heavy For these reasons it is obviously impossible that they could have been worn by cattle or horses, particularly as domestic animals were by all accounts of a slighter build than at present

---

[4] The late Professor Gunnar Tilander helped me with the translation of Violant i Simorra's work from the Catalan.

[5] The late Dr Valdemar Ginters drew my attention to the last two examples.

in the period under consideration. Ulrich Møhl's studies of cattle bones from the ninth to the eleventh century in Viborg demonstrate that cattle were similar to today's Jersey breed (Møhl 1968, comparative table) The large cow-bells which have more recently been used in the Swiss Alps are not relevant in this context as these cattle are much larger (see for instance Gauchet 1909)

It is therefore necessary to look for other uses for these bells. In an earlier account of the Mästermyr find in 1953 I suggested that they could have been processional bells of the kind seen on the Bayeaux tapestry where choirboys holding large bells walk round the bier of Edward the Confessor as he is carried to his burial place in the newly-built Westminster Abbey (Stenton 1957 fig. 32, pll VII; Berg 1955, p. 81). Similar representations can be seen on an Irish reliquary and a gravestone (in the National Museum, Dublin) The use of hand-bells at funerals ended in Sweden with the Reformation (Bringéus 1958 pp. 250f.) J P Joensen has pointed out a more recent parallel from the Faeroes: 'In Hastarvík on Fugloy it is said that in the past a man would walk in front of the coffin and ring a handbell during the journey from the home to the churchyard. In this district there was a churchyard but no church (Joensen 1980, p. 200)

The suggestion that the bells from Mästermyr could have been used for liturgical purposes presupposes that they belong to a period when Christianity had already reached Gotland. Certainly the discovered traces of stave churches at Hemse, Guldrupe and Silte (Trotzig 1972) suggest that this could have happened as early as the eleventh century There is no evidence to suggest that the ringing of bells dates back to pre-Christian times. Lithberg's quotation from Saxo describing how Starkodder in Old Uppsala became enfeebled by '*mollia nolarum crepitacula* can hardly be used as evidence in this context cf. Bringéus 1958, p. 19)

The cauldrons

The three cauldrons from Mästermyr (nos. 19–24) provide, in spite of their fragmentary and poor condition, a valuable contribution to our knowledge of copper vessels in the Viking Age and early medieval period. Traces of soot demonstrate that they were definitely used for cooking, at least at a late stage of their useful life, and it would seem that at the time of the find one of them contained something which may have been traces of food, although this deposit was unfortunately not analysed. The handles indicate that they were suspended over the fire. The method of manufacture was

that of chasing against a hard support leaving a thickness of metal (according to Trotzig's terminology 1978) The two fairly well-preserved cauldrons are estimated to have held about 13.5 and 7.3 litres This can be compared with the large copper cauldron in the Gokstad find which held an estimated 140 litres (Heyerdahl–Larsen 1979–80, p. 43)

The cauldrons must be regarded as scrap-metal which the smith had acquired for future use, although some of the tools in the find can be regarded as suitable for copper-smithing. They are repaired and worn and are therefore not examples of the smith's own work. It is not known in what form the copper alloy reached the maker whether as ingots or as roughly hammered blanks—long rectangular plates which had to be hammered out into sheets.

Copper vessels used in the preparation of food needed to be well scoured in order to prevent food poisoning through the formation of verdigris.

The find also contained a fragment of another cauldron of sheet-iron (unnumbered)

The griddle

The griddle (no. 18) is of a type particularly common in Viking Age finds in Sweden and Norway The pan rotates on a pin at the end of the handle: this arrangement made it possible to turn the pan with a stick as it rested on a tripod or other type of fire stool and thus distribute the heat from the hearth. Griddles come in various sizes and with or without raised rims. In the case of the latter at least, they would primarily have been used for making bread. These griddles must not, however be mistaken for the *takkor* described by Sigurd Grieg (Grøn 1927 p. 56ff. Olaus Magnus 1555 13·16; Grieg 1928, p. 139) These were used for clap-bread and were of cast-iron and completely different in appearance. The griddles were used for thicker bread or buns and those with rims perhaps also for pancakes. Griddles which rotate on a pin in the handle were among the common kitchen equipment of rural Sweden until more recent times (Keyland 1919 pp. 197ff Campbell 1950, pp. 125ff.)

The steelyard

The steelyard (no. 1) from Mästermyr is the only complete example from Scandinavia before the medieval period. However weights from similar objects have been encountered in Viking Age finds from Gotland and in an early medieval find in Lund (Jansson 1936, p. 18

Zachrisson 1962, p. 208, *Uppgrävt förflutet* 1976, p. 191 cf. Jansson 1945). There are many parallels in Central Europe from the Late Roman and Merovingian periods (Paret 1939· Behrens 1939).

The bar of the steelyard would originally have had engraved gradations on two sides. This would have allowed the steelyard to be used in two ways, held either by the ring which still remains attached or by the other ring, which has now broken off. The latter ring was attached a little further away from the hook, where traces of its attachment are still visible. Without knowing the gradations and the suspension points for the goods nothing can be surmised about the units of weight used. The weight of the counterpoise is irrelevant in this context.

The steelyard is suitable for weighing heavier goods and is practical for travellers, as no set of loose weights need be carried. For this reason it became the most common weighing device in more recent times in large parts of Europe and England, while in Sweden, the bismar of eastern origin, remained in use for a long time (Jansson 1952)

The trace-rings

The two pairs of iron rings with attachment loops (nos 87–90) seemed very puzzling at first. However in a paper (1946) Bertil Almgren drew attention to a type of harness for four-wheeled carts, once common in southern Scandinavia and the Baltic area, but also illustrated on one of the tapestries in the Norwegian find from Oseberg (Almgren 1946) [6] A trace of cord or chain was secured at one end to the front axle of the cart outside the nave and at the other to a ring in the horse's harness.

Two finds of such rings have been made in Skåne: the first, from the eighth century in Lackalänge, and the second, from the eleventh century in Nosaby in which case chain fragments are attached to the rings (Strömberg 1961 pl. 51:6–7). Two ring finds from Hillerslev and Søllested, Fyn, Denmark also have iron chains attached. Both finds date from the tenth century (Brøndsted 1936, pp. 143f.).

Helmut Hagar further developed Almgren s account by fitting this harness detail into a larger cultural and geographical context (Hagar 1973 cf also Hagar 1970). The identification of the objects as trace-rings must now be considered to be definite.

Metalwork: iron and steel

Several of the tools in the find were used for iron smithing.

The anvil and the bellows were part of the smithy's fixtures, but smaller pieces were evidently carried by the itinerant blacksmith. The three anvils in the find (nos. 72–74) are similar in appearance to those still used in the last century in western Dalarna. They are unusually small and light, and it is doubtful whether they could have been used without being somehow fitted in an anvil block. However a small anvil of the same type can be seen in Jost Amman s sixteenth-century illustration of a needle-marker (reproduced, for instance, in Oldeberg 1966 fig. 433) Such anvils were usually made by the smiths themselves, their greatest problem being to steel the striking face. The atypically cyndrical piece (no. 74) is perhaps a blank for such an anvil. Beak-irons were also important tools. the find includes two, one larger and one smaller (nos. 75–76) Later examples demonstrate that they were driven into a wooden block when in use. As large anvils did not at this time have beaks these irons were indispensable for lighter work, such as bending rods.[7]

There are a number of sledge hammers and smithing hammers in the find. The term sledge hammer refers to the tools with which an assistant struck a piece of work or another tool, like a chisel, held by the smith. There are three sledge hammers (nos. 69–71) of which the two smaller weigh about 1.85 kg and 1.6 kg. Modern sledge hammers weigh between 2.5 kg and 6 kg. The sledge hammers in the find should perhaps therefore more correctly be defined as large hammers. According to their weight, sledge hammers are distinguished as large sledge hammers and flatteners. Both are wielded with both hands.

The hand hammers (nos 65–67), which were used by the blacksmith himself are of varying sizes but similar designs. They weigh between 0.4 kg and 0.75 kg (compared to 0.8 kg–1.5 kg today) (Hellner and Rooth 1960 p. 260) There are many close parallels to these among smiths tools of later periods although a number of types have developed for specific uses cf. e.g. Tobiassen 1981 pp. 34 ff.)

The two tongs (nos. 43–44) are not rebated, a feature which became common later in the medieval period (Andersen, Crabb and Madsen 1971 p. 246) The complete larger tong (no. 44) is in all other respects generally comparable to more recent smithing tongs. The

---

[6] Other hypotheses on the uses of these rings have subsequently appeared: Carl-Axel Moberg suggests the possibility that they were rubbing tools used in tanning (Moberg 1955, p. 114)!

[7] Nils Hjalmar Matsson argues against Horst Ohlhaver who, he believes, places too much emphasis on the use of beak-irons in plate work (*Lima och Transtrand* 1982, pp. 228 f.).

other (no. 43) is too fragmentary for its purpose to be more closely identified.

The nail-making iron (no. 86) belongs to the standard equipment of the smithy It was used in the manufacture of rivets and nails: the forged blank was inserted in one of the holes and the head was shaped by hammering. Nail-making irons were sometimes made entirely from steel, but usually only the top is steeled. Many medieval illustrations show a blacksmith holding an iron in one hand and leaning it against an anvil.

Two rings (nos. 77–78) served as underlays to protect the anvil when holes were made. They are paralleled in other Viking Age finds, such as the remarkable smith s grave from Bygland, Morgedal, Telemark (Blindheim 1963). This object is known in Gotland as a *lockring* (Klintberg, *Anteckningar*), a term known as early as the seventeenth century (Möllerheim, *Handbok*)

There are two rasps (nos 37–38) and four files (nos. 32–35), of which one is round (no. 34). The latter all have single-graded cuts which, judging from later practice, were produced with a chisel, after which the file was hardened with the aid of pulverised horn cf. e.g. Frost 1941 p. 47) It is tempting to suggest that the small piece of elk antler (no. 128) is evidence that this method of hardening was used. The use of pulverised horn to harden files was already recommended by Theophilus 1933 III, 11). The hack-saw (no. 36) is directly comparable with such tools in recent sets of tools (cf. e.g. Tobiassen 1981 p. 42).[8] Andreas Oldeberg has pointed out that the files in the Mästermyr find, which have rectangular square and round sections, represent all the known types of these tools from the late Iron Age (Oldeberg 1966 p. 121 on the rasps, cf van Tyghen 1966 p. 54).

Several of the tools described here could also have been used in other metalwork, such as copper-smithing. This is the case with the small anvils, especially the beak-irons and with some of the hammers, particularly no. 71 which could have been used as a flat hammer for making metal sheets, a so-called planishing hammer The stretching hammer (no. 68) was also used for working both iron and copper sheets.

The tongs (no. 44), the hacksaw (no. 36) and the plate-shears (no. 45) were also used for work in sheet metal, and the plate-shears are of a type common among smiths' tools until the present day

It is curious that such a common tool as the sett is missing from this find: this is a kind of chisel with which the hot iron was severed. However there is a cold drill

(no. 52) with which a hole could be made in cold iron. The drill was greased to prevent undue friction and was struck with the sledge hammer The tools (nos. 104–105) have neither edges nor peens and are therefore difficult to identify It is possible that they are damaged setts. Setts, like cold drills were held wedged in wooden handles in use, or had handles made of withes wound round the iron.

Metalwork. metals other than iron

There is considerable evidence to suggest that the craftsman who left his tools in Mästermyr did not only work in iron. The unworked cake of brass (no. 127) seems to indicate that he also engaged in copper smithing, as do the cauldrons of copper alloy which were the raw material for new products

If Greta Arwidsson is correct in suggesting that the two tripod stands (nos. 92a–93) served as supports for crucibles, it would seem that casting metal presumably bronze or copper—was another of the smith s tasks Other tools in the collection are worth considering in this context.

Andreas Oldeberg has interpreted as a soldering lamp the boat-shaped object with sharp shanks (no. 56) which were obviously intended to be set in a wooden block (Oldeberg 1966, p. 71) An object of similar appearance has since been discovered during excavation of a habitation deposit in Lund, dated to the second half of the twelfth century (*Uppgrävt förflutet* 1976, pp. 202 ff.). Anders Mårtensson, who published the find, agrees with Oldeberg's identification. Both authors refer to soldering lamps used by silver smiths. in these lamps the high flame produced by ox-tallow and a rag wick was directed with a blow-pipe to the point which was to be soldered (Bengtsson 1945 pp. 238 f.) However these lamps do not have the striking long, narrow shape of the Mästermyr object.

The iron spatula (no. 102) was presumably also used for soldering copper and other similar metals. A similar object was found in 1966 in the material from medieval Lund, and can be dated by its context to the second half of the eleventh century (Mårtensson 1972, pp. 128 ff.) Spatulas of this type also occur among the tools from Helgö (Tomtlund 1978, p. 16) During soldering, the tool could have been used to sprinkle the fluxing agent (usually pulverised borax) on the joint, thus preventing oxidation while the hard solder was applied. At a later date a special can was used for this purpose, the borax being dispensed at a suitable rate through a spout at the bottom. Known as a *boraxfass* it occurs from the

---

[8] With reference to the files, Arne Skjølsvold has warned against identifying them as exclusively smiths' tools, on the basis of Norwegian finds (Skjølsvold 1969, p. 175).

second half of the fifteenth century (Bengtsson 1945 pp. 237 f. Bengtsson 1973)

The polishing iron (no. 53) could also have been used in connection with soldering. Copper- and silversmiths' standard equipment usually included a steel tool for this purpose. However similar tools were also used to smooth both forged and soldered joints in farm smithies

One of the hammers (no. 68) is of a type known more recently as a stretching hammer Its presence would suggest that the Mästermyr smith also produced vessels probably of bronze. The characteristic feature of this tool is the position of the haft-hole near one end, facilitating its use even in fairly deep vessels. In more recent times this tool was primarily used for the manufacture of copper or copper alloy vessels (cf. Trotzig 1978). However as its purpose is to reach the bottom of deep vessels, it could equally well be used for vessels made of sheet-iron.

In this context the stamp punch (no. 84) and the stamping pad of lead (no. 85) should be remembered, as the punch could only have been used on precious metal or copper alloys.

Two long narrow pieces of iron (nos. 79–80) with punched holes, some of which perforate the iron while others stop short of complete penetration, have been identified in the archaeological literature as drawplates, used to produce metal wire. Andreas Oldeberg, however restricts his identification to draw-plate or possibly nail-making iron (Oldeberg 1966 fig. 79–80) This group of tools has been the subject of extensive and rather confused discussion in the past.[9] The draw-plates used more recently to make wire do not convincingly resemble the archaeological artefacts. Draw-plates are distinguished from nail-making irons in that the former have a series of holes of diminishing sizes. The nail-making irons used when making horseshoe nails in particular normally have fewer holes, and these of the same size. As the anvil had no holes for this purpose, such a tool was necessary The draw-plates must have been set in a bench or stool (e.g. as represented in a copper-plate engraving from the fifteenth century Bengtsson 1945, pp. 191 235). The wire was pulled by hand, lubricated by some sort of grease, a method later replaced by the use of a hand-driven wheel. A seminal study of wire-drawing was produced by Jorma Leppäaho in 1949. There are no later examples of draw-plates of the type found at Mästermyr (on wire-drawing, cf *Lima och Transtrand* 1982, p.

271 f. where the draw-plates illustrated are certainly prehistoric)

The holes in the (?)draw-plates from Mästermyr do not, however penetrate the iron. They cannot therefore be regarded as suitable for this purpose. Nor can they be nail-making irons, as these also require perforations. We can only surmise that these are uncompleted pieces of work.

The Smith

The chest was discovered near the edge of the former lake or swamp Eske träsk, which was part of the large complex of swamps and marshland known as Mästermyr drained at the beginning of this century The name Mästermyr is of unknown origin. A plausible interpretation would be the 'great marsh but there are linguistic objections to this (Gustavson 1938 p. 17 personal communication, Professor Ingmar Olsson) [10]

The site is remote and, particularly before draining, unsuitable for the deposition of a hoard. nor was the chest an object of great value. It is more likely therefore, that the find is the result of some kind of accident, or perhaps a desire to conceal a criminal act such as murder or theft.

The objects in the find must in any case be seen as belonging to a single craftsman. The most obvious suggestion is that he lost his tools while travelling from one place of work to another It is not likely that he went by boat. A narrow and unstable boat known as an *äska* was used in the area for fishing; it was not rowed, but punted along with a pole in the shallow waters (Ljungqvist 1906, pp. 221f.) The accident probably happened in the winter but did not necessarily involve loss of life. Ice forms in these areas at the beginning of January and breaks up in early April.

When I enquired whether it was possible that a regular winter road across Mästermyr had existed in the past, serving to shorten travelling distances between the settlements round the marsh, an authority on these conditions, Rolf Hildebrand, former Director of Gotland's Highways Board, answered with the following statement:

Our climatic conditions do not permit, and can still less be imagined to have permitted in the Viking Age, the building of regular winter roads across the ice, such as are found in central or northern Sweden. However I think it likely that

---

[9] On the discussion of draw-plates and nail-making irons see particularly Grieg 1920–22, pp. 60 ff. and Petersen 1951 pp. 98 ff.

[10] Wilhelm Holmqvist imagines that this wide tract was named after the smith who left the chest behind in the marsh: 'The name Mästermyr can be taken as evidence of how the surrounding people considered him' (Holmqvist 1979, p. 49)!

during and after snowstorms any ice in the swamps, blown free of snow would have been used in preference to the roads in the surrounding area which would have been made almost impassable by snowdrifts. Although the swamps have now more or less disappeared, the risk of drifting in these places still persists and has to be prevented with snow screens. But when the sea is iced up and there is a snowstorm, the problem of drifting becomes acute; snowscreens can offer no protection from that direction. The short-legged Gotland pony (*russ*) would have had great difficulties in such places particularly with an iron chest on its back. (Letter 21 August 1979.)

Hildebrand evidently suggest the possibility that the chest was loaded on a pack-horse. Although this might have been the case, it is equally likely that the chest was carried on a sledge. However no traces of a sledge were found. Whatever the means of transport, it is obvious that the bronze cauldrons and the large bells were tied to the outside of the chest.

The risk of such accidents occurring was presumably considerable. Evidence of this is found in a provision among the testamentory depositions of the Uppland Law a provincial law established in 1296, which was for a long time the norm for legislation throughout Sweden. This provision ruled that if a family travelling in one sledge was drowned all at the same time, the heirs of the man would inherit from him, and the heirs of the woman from her (Collin-Schlyter 1834, pp. 121f.)

We can only guess at the direction in which the man with the chest and the other objects was travelling. When standing on the old bed of Eske träsk, the spires of Silte and Sproge churches appear like lighthouses on the horizon. But we do not know by what means the men of the Viking Age found their way between, say Hallvards in Silte and Stymnes or Bosarve and Sproge. Many finds testify that at this time these were rich settlements. It may also be pointed out that if the spoon-augers and some other tools in the find were associated with boat-building the itinerant craftsman must have worked over a wider area. The key-handle of spruce (no. 3) must have been made north of Mästermyr since the southern boundary of spruce at present, and evidently also in the past, runs between Silte and Sproge (Sernander 1939· cf. von Post in Munthe, Hede and von Post 1927 p. 135· 'Pollen diagrams from Mästermyr and from sites in the south clearly show that this boundary has been maintained since the definitive migration of the spruce').

*

In his seminal study of *Smedsverktøi i norske gravfund* (Smiths tools in Norwegian grave finds) Sigurd Grieg ends by posing the question. were there village blacksmiths in the Viking Age? He answered the question in the affirmative after a certain amount of deliberation (Grieg 1920, pp. 92f.) However Grieg touched only briefly on conditions in later periods, and it is for this reason that the question must be considered in a wider context. First, we need to know how common it was for every farm to have a smithy Anna Helene Tobiassen has demonstrated that this varied greatly through Norway's history (Tobiassen 1981 pp. 4 ff.) In Sweden there is a clear distinction between the practice in Skåne and the rest of the country While in most provinces it was the norm for all well-appointed farms to have a smithy in a special building, in Skåne, and often also in the other former Danish provinces it was usual to find a common village or parish smithy There was also a blacksmith, paid by the people of the village, just as there was a herdsman to look after the livestock.

This does not imply that in those parts of the country where farms had their own smithies there were no professional blacksmiths As a rule only simpler smithing tasks could be performed by the men on the farms while more extensive and complicated work was undertaken by specialist craftsmen who, like tailors and cobblers worked for one or more days as guest workers on the farms A large body of material provides evidence of the firm rules and customs which attached to these visits. Fixtures in the smithy particularly the anvil and bellows must be in good condition when the blacksmith came to the farm, there must be a supply of charcoal, which the farmer must burn himself and assistance must be provided by the farmer or someone in his employ for wielding the sledge hammer and operating the bellows. It appears that the smith did not bring journeymen or apprentices, contrary to the custom of other craftsmen. The blacksmith was often a farmer who practised his craft as a part-time occupation, perhaps primarily in the winter These conditions only changed in the middle of the nineteenth century when the blacksmith became a full-time craftsman with a smithy of his own to which his customers would travel.

In Skåne and adjacent former Danish provinces the situation was quite different and can be seen to date back to the medieval period. Here, there would generally be a smithy near every parish church, with a blacksmith paid by the villagers. According to the Lund diocese landbook of about 1580, the smithy was either owned by the church or built by the villagers and let to the church (Ljunggren 1965 pp. 14 f.) Rudolf Zeitler has pointed out that the building of the first stone churches already required the services of technically skilled blacksmiths who could 'keep the drill-bits in shape so that they cut well a village smith—a farmer who spent most of his time keeping the iron tools of the village in good condition (Zeitler 1977–78 p. 119).

Medieval legislation recognised the existence of craftsmen who were not landowners, but this must have been exceptional, and even the Skåne blacksmith had a small parcel of land at his disposal, even though he did not own it (cf. Granlund 1944, Hanssen 1953 pp. 493 ff.) The social structure which included village blacksmiths was necessarily based on Continental patterns and was perhaps ultimately the result of urbanisation, which made for a greater diversification in society and a greater specialisation in work (cf. Lindberg 1947 pp. 17 ff.). In Sweden also this tendency obviously had an early effect on the organisation of the crafts in towns and the staff of palaces and manors.

We must imagine, therefore, that the Mästermyr smith probably belonged to the category of *gångande gärningsmän* (itinerant craftsmen) to borrow an expression from the medieval provincial laws. He brought with him the movable equipment which was used together with the fixtures of the farm smithy Many place-names containing *Smed* (in Gotland *Smiss* testify that there were many like him in the early Viking Age and early medieval period (Calissendorff 1979 pp. 166 f.).

Woodwork

Several tools in the find demonstrate that the smith also worked with wood.

The most important of these are the two axes (nos. 61–62) and the two adzes (nos. 63–64). The axes differ in size and in some details. Both specimens are of the type with two flanges at the haft-holes but without any incipient ridge on the underside of the necks cf. Thålin-Bergman 1976) This type of axe is a universal tool; it is shown on the Bayeux tapestry for instance, used for felling trees. It is also possible that it was used as a wedge to split tree trunks into half-logs and planks, this was the method in common use before the introduction of the long saw (pit-saw) cf. Berg 1958)

Adzes are uncommon in the Viking Age finds. The T-shaped adze, with its broad curved edge, is particularly noteworthy This tool was used to smooth the surface of the split planks before they were fitted, for use as boat planking, for instance. Balks of timber for house building were then, as later smoothed with broad axes However adze marks are not infrequently found in medieval timber buildings and furniture (for Norwegian examples see Liestøl 1976, col. 650) But the common use of this tool became very rare as early

as the medieval period, largely through the increased use of the saw It continued to be used in coopering, where, with a curved edge, it was used to smooth the insides of the casks. Another specialised use was in the making of gutters.

Apart from the hack-saw (no. 36) which belongs with the metalwork tools, there are two saws in the find. One is a kind of handsaw of unusual type (no. 42) The filing of the teeth from opposite sides in groups of three or four is apparently unique, according to W L. Goodman 1964, p. 123) This saw has a handle, but the small saw-blade (no. 41) has none, in this case the teeth are filed and set normally

It is most unusual for a tool find of this type to contain such a large collection of spoon-augers (nos. 46–51 unfortunately all without handles. These tools provide the most important indication that this craftsman also practised boat-building.

Augers like these could have had a variety of handles They often had a loop at the end through which a straight handle was inserted to turn the auger In other examples the top was inserted in a horizontal or wing-shaped handle, but in these cases the auger was usually offset, to prevent it penetrating the handle. As these features are missing here, the augers can best be reconstructed on the model of breast-augers where the central handle is movable and has a fixed button at the top: the craftsman leaned on the button, driving the auger down by the weight of his body while at the same time turning it with the handle. This ingenious device is very old and occurred very widely In the Bayeux tapestry we see a boat-builder working away with an auger and similar scenes are represented in some later medieval illustrations (Goodman 1964, pp. 172 f van Tyghen 1966, p. 32, Leppäaho 1951) The iron collars encircling the handles at the bottom, of which four are preserved (nos. 98–101) confirm that these augers were indeed of this type.

The augers in the find are remarkably slight, the bits varying in width from 0.7 cm to 1.9 cm. For simpler boring in wood, the transverse handle was commonly used rather than the breast-auger This was also the case where an auger was used for reamering out the hubs of wheels, a use which gave the auger its common Swedish name *navare* (sw *nav* = hub Jorma Leppäaho is probably correct to emphasise the use of the fully developed breast-auger primarily as a tool associated with boat-building; this use was certainly widespread. In clinker-built boats holes had to be bored to take the rivets. The auger was very well suited to this task, particularly as it could be used in a variety of angles and positions. The small dimensions of the Mästermyr examples were probably not unsuitable for this purpose. The use of augers in Viking Age ship-building was demonstrated during the investigation of the Skuldelev ships, sunk near the coast of Sjælland. Some holes which for structural reasons did not penetrate the wood, had the characteristic rounded bottoms left by the auger (Olsen and Crumlin-Pedersen 1967 pl. 61)

Breast-augers were also used to bore holes in cross trees on thatched roofs. Their use for this purpose gave them the name *malkuri* in some Finnish dialects in Österbotten, a name already found in medieval texts (Valonen 1951). The wooden spars which were laid near the roof-ridge on reed-thatched roofs on Gotland were joined in the same manner (observed in Lau by Mathias Klintberg; Klintberg and Gustavson 1972, see *Navare*).

The moulding-iron (no. 57) is not common in Swedish finds, but has many parallels in Norway where it has been used in boat-building up to the present day especially to decorate the gunwale. The tool could be drawn in both directions hence the three symmetrical cutting edges on each side of the central support. The moulding is in this case very simple, rather like that on the Norwegian boat from Karmøy Rogaland (see *Kulturhistoriskt lexikon för nordisk medeltid, Profil*) More complicated mouldings occur in other finds from the Viking Age and medieval period, such as the boat find from Årby Uppland (Arbman 1940, pp. 38 f.) Mouldings of this type also occur on furniture and buildings (Krog and Voss 1961 pp. 27 f see also *Kulturhistoriskt lexikon for nordisk medeltid, Profil*)

The two shanks of the moulding-iron fitted in a wooden handle, of which no traces remain. This was also the case with the draw-knives (nos. 54–55) which were used to hollow out pieces of wood to make troughs or vessels of various kinds. Many finds from the Viking Age and early medieval period demonstrate the importance of vessels made from single pieces of wood. Up until the present day sets of tools in rural areas commonly include draw-knives intended for this purpose. It is sometimes stated in the archaeological literature that they were used for smoothing wood surfaces, such as boat planks, but this cannot be confirmed, the broad axe, or in places where it could not reach, the adze, was used for this purpose, as stated above. Thus the adze was also a boat-builder's tool (Rålamb 1692, p. 44, cf Waagepetersen 1965 17)

Other tools used in carpentry are the gouge and the chisel. It has already been suggested that the gouge (no. 58) could have been used to make the rabbets which were part of the joints between the bottom and sides of the chest. The gouge would also be used to take up the mortices in the sides in which the tenons of the bottom fitted. As in later periods this was done by boring two holes with an auger and enlarging these to a rectangular

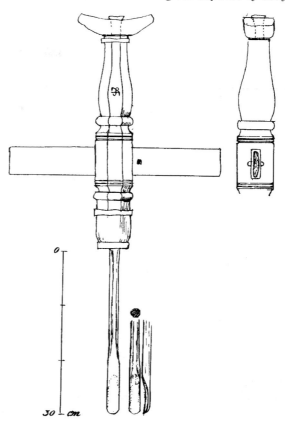

Fig. 4. An auger from the collections of Nordiska Museet, catalogue number 195870.

shape with a gouge. The chisel (no. 59) with its flared edge (known on Sollerö as a *skjutjärn* was used for similar purposes (for this type, cf van Tyghen 1966, p. 42)

The small tool (no. 96) with its cloven edge and ash handle, has not been identified. Oldeberg 1966, p. 71) interprets it as 'possibly a *brännjärn*

It is possible that the four files and two rasps (nos. 32–35 37–38) were also used for carpentry but they have been considered with the smiths tools above (p. 31)

However the small whetstone (no. 123) obviously belongs with the carpentry tools and was used to sharpen the cutting edges.

There is no definite evidence that the Mästermyr smith also practised coopering. Draw-knives could, as we have seen, be used for other purposes as well, indeed draw-knife no. 54 has a rather straight edge, while a more curved edge would have been more practical for work inside a cask. Other tools connected with this craft are missing, such as the stave iron and hoop hook. In his study of coopering technique, Dag Trotzig identifies no. 58 as a *skjutjärn*, a curved gouge, used to

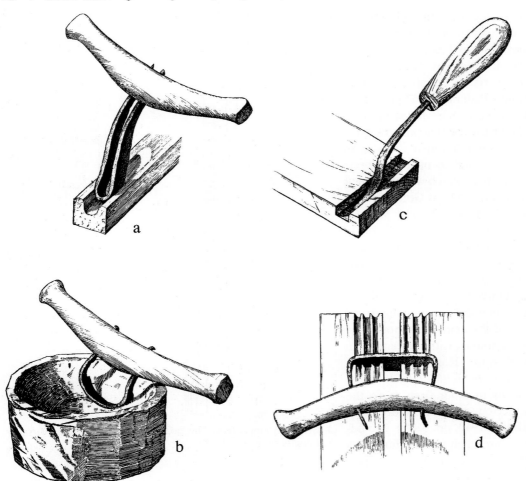

Fig. 5. Carpenters tools from the collections of Nordiska Museet: a–b) draw-knives, c) a gouge, d) a moulding iron.

make the groove at the bottom of the cask, which was first marked out with the scribing knife. He quotes a parallel from a Norwegian Viking Age find (Trotzig 1938, p. 348 f.). Trotzig demonstrated that an angular groove is an early feature in coopering. The casks in the Oseberg find already have bevelled edges and simpler grooves. However as we have seen, the gouge could also have been used for other purposes, such as producing the rabbets joining the bottom of the chest to the sides.

5. The age of the find
by Greta Arwidsson

Despite the large number of objects in the Mästermyr find there are few datable features.

In the first place this is because the tools which make up the main body of the find do not have such features whose variations would enable the establishment of a chronology Collections of tools associated with specific crafts only became common in finds from the Viking Age on; but single tools or small groups of tools, in every way comparable to the Mästermyr examples, do occasionally occur in graves from earlier periods (see chapter 3). This confirms that tools of this type were part of the craftsman s equipment even before the Viking Age, although only rarely have they been preserved other than in graves. For instance, heavier tools are seldom found in excavations of house sites, which suggests that iron would have been carefully salvaged from burnt-out houses for re-use. This was apparently also the case with cremations. gold and bronze fragments from sword hilts and spear-heads etc. are often found in the remains of the pyre, indicating that weapons had been among the grave goods (Arrhenius 1963 cf. Lindqvist 1936, p. 179; Lamm 1962; Åberg 1953 cf. Arrhenius 1972, where the find has not been published in full).[1]

However certain tool types and technical features in the Mästermyr find do suggest a date in the late Viking Age or possibly the early medieval period, although a later date cannot definitely be ruled out.

The padlocks are of particular interest in this context, although the details of their construction cannot be ascertained. Padlocks of similar types are not known in Scandinavia before the Viking Age. However keys apparently designed for use in such locks occur in the Vendel period (Almgren 1942 and 1955) Some of these are imported while others are clearly Scandinavian copies Almgren has emphasised that they were sometimes used as charms, and that their presence does not therefore necessarily indicate that such locks were actually used in Scandinavia at this time.

At Birka padlocks are found both in graves and in settlement deposits near Borg (e.g. graves 523 562 and 737 Arbman s unpublished excavation in 1931) These are of particular interest because of their similarity to the Mästermyr locks which includes technical features. Thus both large and small lock barrels are decorated with soldered-on iron rods twisted finely and evenly (*Birka* I Pl. 273)

A large decorated key with a bronze shank probably belongs to the lock from Birka grave 562, which is decorated in this way However it is difficult to interpret the ornament on the key (cf. Birka, vol. I p. 182, fig. 134)

None of the padlocks from the Birka graves can be accurately dated, since the graves contain few other objects. However it must be remembered that the settlements at Birka seem to be completely abandoned before the year 1000 (Ambrosiani *et al*. 1973 pp. 237–243) and that there are few graves from the Migration and Vendel period settlements (Arrhenius 1976) There was no urban settlement on the island after the Viking Age. The period of settlement is less clearly defined on Helgö, whose workshops apparently produced padlocks. No padlocks were found in the graves there, and the locks produced are apparently dated to the Viking Age, largely on the basis of a comparison with examples from Birka (Tomtlund 1970; see also *Excavations at Helgö* I–II)

The chronological position of the padlocks found in Sweden can be better determined on the basis of recently published material from Århus Søndervold (Andersen *et al*. 1971) and from Novgorod (Kolčin 1959) where locks and keys of the relevant types are found in levels deposited in the tenth and eleventh/twelfth centuries.

Technical details such as the twisted iron rods and faceted nodes of bronze on iron objects – as on the large key (no. 2) and the steelyard (no. 1) from Mästermyr—occurred in Scandinavia before the Viking Age e.g. Arwidsson 1942, Taf. 36, nos. 260, 281 cf. Abb. 78) The technique of plating iron with brass bronze or white metal—as on the bells (nos. 26–28)—was used at least from the Vendel period (Arwidsson 1977 p. 57 *Zeumzeug* II)

An interesting body of comparative material for the large key (no. 2) occurs in Gotland, where numerous keys of similar type and construction have been found.

This suggests an understanding of the fact that iron would be hardened in the strong heat of the pyre, and was therefore sought after for re-use.

The larger keys either have a spool-shaped portion of the shank made up of twisted iron rods with nodes of bronze or brass like the Mästermyr example, or the shank takes the form of a simple loop-bow e.g. Thunmark 1979 153). The latter type seems to have been most common. The keys of the former type which do not unfortunately occur in closed grave finds are of chronological significance, as the shape of the nodes and their punched decoration can be compared to knobs and decoration on annular brooches from Gotland. The upper node on the shank may be faceted and decorated with dot-and-eye motifs (e.g. Gotl. F C 918. A 2220), while in several cases the lower node is shaped like an animal head or—in one case—a human head (e.g. Gotl. F C 918, C 1010, C 2092 and A 3998) The most detailed of these is the gaping head of a wild animal on key C 2092, which may be compared to similar heads on annular brooches like those from Birka graves 477 and 736 (*Birka* I pl. 48:2–3) Grave 736 is definitely from the tenth century while the other grave may be a little earlier

There can be no chronological significance in the fact that the large keys, with spool-shaped shanks of twisted rods or simple loop-bows, never occur in women's graves, which in the Vendel period and Viking Age often contain small keys of a great variety of types (*VZG passim* and Stenberger 1961 fig. 77) It is clear that the large keys were not carried on the bunch of keys and other small implements which women wore, and were thus not part of the collection of personal items which accompanied her in the grave. The size of the keys suggests that they fitted large locks, such as those on doors or large storage chests.

Small keys with spool-shaped handles of iron rods apparently also occurred in Gotland. However only one of these is from a closed grave find (from Ihre, Hellvi Stenberger 1962, no. 133 fig. 77) dated to the tenth century by several items of female jewellery

The type of construction used for the shank of key no. 2 and the spool-shaped part of the steelyard hook (no. 1) is also found on two steelyards both probably from Gotland. There is no information about one of them (SMH inv no. 25177), but the other is a casual find from Bote, Garde (Gotl. F inv no. C 9150). Kolčin (1958, fig. 81 1) has published a hook with a similar construction (perhaps belonging to a steelyard). Unfortunately the dating is uncertain.

Three measures from Birka graves 834, 845 and 660 (*Birka* I, pl. 125:1–3) have spool-shaped handles made from twisted iron rods and bronze nodes, similar to the key no. 2. Faceted bronze nodes decorated with ring-and-dot motifs occur and in one case (grave 660) there is a node shaped like an animal head biting the measuring bar The handle of an object from Søreim, Dale, Sogn og Fjordane, Norway is similar in construction (Petersen 1951 fig. 227) Petersen believes this object to be a roasting spit and states that there are fifteen examples of this type in finds from the Norwegian Viking Age out of a total of forty-eight roasting spits known from this period 1951 p. 427) According to Petersen they can be dated to the ninth and tenth centuries. The measures from Birka come from well-dated women s graves. the earliest is probably from the end of the ninth century and the other two, which include Arabic silver coins struck in 913–932 and 934–943 respectively may be one or two generations later (*Birka* I pp. 304, 319, 231)

However the technique of joining sheets by overlapping and 'stitching' that is inserting the edge of one sheet alternately over and under flaps cut at the edge of the adjoining sheet and securing the join by soldering, as on the bronze cauldrons nos 19 and 23—seems first to have been introduced in Scandinavia in the Viking Age.

The large cauldron from Gokstad (Nicolaysen 1882 and Petersen 1951 fig. 213) like that from the Skopintull' burial mound on Adelsö (Rydh 1936, p. 116 and Trotzig 1978 p. 14) is dated by association to the ninth or tenth centuries.

A group of boxes from Gotland, made by the same method, is dated by the coins they contain to roughly the middle of the eleventh century (Stenberger 1947 fig. 290 no. 524, fig. 291 no. 593 fig. 292 no 356. fig. 229 no. 613 etc.) These coin boxes demonstrate that the technique of joining plates by this method was known on Gotland certainly by the first half of the eleventh century and perhaps earlier (Trotzig 1978)

The fact that earlier coin hoards and certain eleventh-century hoards, were deposited in small wooden boxes e.g. the unpublished hoard from Bjärs in Stenkyrka, Gotland) may indicate that metal boxes were not very common on Gotland before the eleventh century At present it can be neither proved nor disproved that the overlapping and 'stitching' technique was used on Gotland by the tenth century and that bronze boxes existed at this time. There appears to have been no attempt at a systematic differentiation between the techniques of the earliest examples and those of medieval and later times (Oldeberg 1966, p. 126; Trotzig 1978, p. 15)

The chest itself and its technical details can perhaps also be used for dating purposes. The dating of the oak timber by dendrochronology should be possible but has not so far been attempted. A dendrochronological series for Gotland is still only in the planning stage.

The chest exemplifies a type of construction which

may be compared to other buried examples, the difficulty being that in many cases only traces of wood remain.

Viking graves have produced a large number of small chests and boxes, such as those from the cemeteries at Birka (*Birka* I, Taf. 259–267). As a rule these boxes can be locked and have carefully-worked hasps and handles for carrying. In some cases they have hinges in some ways similar to those on the Mästermyr chest, but they often have ordinary hinge joints (*Birka* I pl. 259–269) The boxes and small chests were usually at least joined with metal mounts and nails Details of their construction are unfortunately unclear as only very little of the wood is preserved. In some cases there is evidence of domed lids and inward-slanting ends e.g. *Birka* I, pl. 263).

The most common types among the numerous coffins from the Birka cemeteries are rectangular and trapezoid coffins joined with large iron nails (Gräslund 1980, pp. 15–20). Where known, the wood is oak. Nailed coffins of this type are also found very frequently in other Scandinavian cemeteries of the late Viking Age cf. Zachrisson 1958)

A Viking Age coffin, assembled without any metal parts, was found in the cemetery on Mora äng, Lagga, Uppland (SMH inv no. 22289 Holmgren 1933 Zachrisson 1958 p. 195) The proportions of this coffin differ from the Mästermyr chest—it is 211 cm long, 44 cm wide and at least 40 cm high at the ends—but it is similar in that the ends continue below the bottom to form 'feet' 7 cm high. The bottom fits into transverse rabbets in the ends while the sides are butted against the bottom plank and pegged to the ends. The lid is ridged or perhaps domed. Interesting features are the depressions cut in the ends which served as hand-holds when the coffin was lifted. This find cannot be dated more accurately than to the late Viking Age. Several nailed wooden coffins were found nearby in similar graves very few of these contained datable finds.[2]

A large number of coffins from the early medieval period are now known. They vary greatly in form and construction and I have been unable to find any close parallels to the Mästermyr chest in the published material (Zachrisson 1958, Blomqvist & Mårtensson 1963 Mårtensson 1976 and Andersen *et al.* 1971)

Large storage chests are included in the well-dated Oseberg find (*Oseberg* vol. II) The closest parallel to the Mästermyr chest is perhaps the simplest of these (fig. 68, no. 178). It is thus evident that this kind of construction was used in the early Viking Age and there are reasons to believe that it was used even earlier (see Gösta Berg, The chest)

When it becomes possible to carry out dendrochronological and C^{14} analyses it is, however not to be expected that these will provide a very accurate date for the tool types or contribute to an estimate of the date of deposition. Old timber may have been re-used to make this simple chest, and it would appear quite possible that it was not originally intended for use as a toolchest. The elaborate locking mechanism suggests that it had previously been used to store more precious possessions It may have been discarded because of the damage which evidently occurred in antiquity (see description in the catalogue)

Metallurgical and metallographical analyses of the iron may eventually identify technical variations which may influence the determination of the area and date of production (Appendix II) Current research projects on iron at metallographical centres in Scandinavia and elsewhere have already yielded most important results suggesting that analyses of such an important find complex as that from Mästermyr would be most desirable. But there is another way of looking at this question. it may be advisable to wait until improved research methods, and the concomitant improvement in the interpretation of results have progressed even further before taking more samples from this material. From the point of view of such research, the tools from Mästermyr are of much less primary value than the well-stratified finds from such larger deposits as those found in the towns which emerged in the Viking Age like Lund, Haithabu, Ribe, Århus and Novgorod (Blomqvist & Mårtensson 1963· Mårtensson 1976; Jankuhn 1943 and 1956; Bencard 1979· Andersen, Crabb & Madsen 1971 Kolčin 1959)

Two objects have long been considered to be of chronological significance: the stamp punch (no. 84) and the stamping pad of lead (no. 85) which carries several triangular impressions. The punch is so badly damaged that it cannot now be ascertained whether this was the tool which made the impressions in the lead pad. These impressions are very sharp and reveal three raised dots in each triangle. This motif is well represented in the Viking Age and occurs quite frequently on silver jewellery from Gotland (Stenberger 1958 p. 288 1962, no. 133 and Thunmark 1974, p. 30; cf also Hårdh

---

[2] Zachrisson's opinion that the construction of the coffin from Mora äng is the same as the coffins from St Lars in Linköping and others, also described by him (1958), is erroneous. Unpublished detailed drawings of the ends show no traces of the mortices for the tenons of the bottom plank or of the wedges which supposedly locked ends and bottom plank together The depression cut into the end above the level of the bottom plank has nothing to do with a mortice and tenon construction. The coffin was examined carefully by Greta Arwidsson when it was moved to Uppsala University archaeological laboratory and no traces of iron nails could then be observed.

1976 B, e.g. Taf. 1.I, 3 16:I 9 and 19 3) The threedot-triangle also occurs on bronze objects such as a couple of mounts from knife-sheathes from tenth-century graves in the cemetery at Ire/Hellvi (Stenberger 1962, ños. 124 and 135). This type of stamped decoration is found on objects in hoards dated to the tenth century but also in later finds, such as the large annular brooch in the hoard from Sigsarve/Hejde, which was probably deposited about 1050–1060 (Stenberger 1947 232 1958 p. 106).

In a study of gold bracteates, P.-O Bohlin discusses this triangular stamp motif (1981 p. 126, fig. 213) He discerns a distinct difference between earlier stamps, which feature a triangular frame round the three dots and Viking Age stamps, which produce the triangle as a flat depressed area round the raised dots In Gotland, bracteates decorated with the latter type of stamped ornament occur in several finds (e.g. *VZG* pl. 273 no. 2199 pl. 274 no. 2209 and pl. 275 no. 2223 which Nerman refers to the end of the Vendel period, period VII.5 while Stenberger 1958 pp. 117 121 refers them to the early Viking Age)

The stamp punch and the stamping pad cannot be dated more accurately than 'probably to the Viking Age We must therefore conclude that these objects are of little value in determining the age of the tool find.

Appendix I
Geological analysis of the Mästermyr site
by Gösta Lundqvist †

Introduction

The island of Gotland consists mainly of Silurian lime-stones and marlstones. A grey fairly fine-grained sandstone (the Burgsvik sandstone) occurs on top of these in the south of the island. The action of the ice on these fine-grained rocks produced the highly calcareous till which is the most important arable soil in Gotland. The melt water of the ice and the wave action of the Baltic have also produced gravel and sand. It is difficult to establish whether sand and gravel deposits are primary or secondary since most of the glacio-fluvial deposits have been extensively redeposited by wave washing.

About 9.6 % of Gotland's area is occupied by water-logged ground, mostly fens. Raised bogs are very rare, presumably because species of *Sphagnum* cannot tolerate the high lime content. Even such *Sphagnum* species as typically occur in fens are rare in Gotland. The undrained fens were characterised by *Cladium mariscus* (cut-sedge, known in Sweden as *Gotlandsag* with some *Carex* species, *Schoenus nigricans S ferrugineus* etc.

Gotland's climate is maritime: winters are normally relatively mild while the summers are not particularly hot. The Baltic serves as a levelling heat reservoir Precipitation is low· approximately 450 mm per year It is not clear how much of it falls as snow but the autumn rains account for a relatively large proportion of the annual precipitation. The water-table is high in the autumn and winter This is of the greatest significance for the development of the fens and their vegetation. This annual distribution of high water phases represents a major difference between the fens and lakes of Gotland and those on the mainland.

Mästermyr

According to Ljungqvist (1914, p. 1), Mästermyr used to be the largest continuous fen in Gotland. It covered 2350 hect. divided into 1996 hect. of fen, 274 hect. of swamps, ponds and pools and 80 hect. of meadows and holms within the fen. It may seem strange to quote figures based on Sylvan (1892) but present-day conditions are so altered by draining and cultivation that more reliable information is difficult to obtain (see also analyses of sections from Snoder Lundqvist 1965 p. 23ff.)

Vegetation

Mästermyr was drained between 1902 and 1910 and is now largely under cultivation. Its present appearance gives no indication of its original state. The following data are therefore based entirely on von Post (1927) and Ljungqvist (1914) Pl. 31;2. The fen included several larger or smaller islands of firm ground and a number of swamps and groups of small pools known locally as *punsar* (where these occur in Martebo *myr* in the north of Gotland they are known as *norar*) The fen was divided according to the predominant vegetation (rather than the thickness of the peat layer) into two zones. the central fen area and the marginal *lagg* which had only a thin layer of peat and formed a transitional zone between the fen and the firm ground. The width of the *lagg* round the edges of the fen and the islands varied, but was normally about 100 m. Along some of the banks of the swamps there were raised ridges.

In addition to these general remarks certain features can be described in more detail.

Cladium mariscus is known in Sweden as *Gotlandsag* because it is so common in the Gotland fens It is a sedge which grows to a height of 2 m and has sharp, saw-edged leaves with the unpleasant property of lacerating anybody who attempts to walk through it. Indeed, it is not possible to walk through it, as the stalks have to be pressed down and the feet slid across the resultant closely-packed mattress. It is typical of *Cladium* that it spreads concentrically· large communities therefore consist of several round patches of up to 20–30 cm in diameter It requires a maritime climate with relatively mild winters to prevent frost-damage to the shoots.

Cladium was most widespread in the eastern and southern parts of the fen where the peat cover is thickest.

The central area of the eastern part of the fen, east of Nydträsk and south of Tunngans träsk, was also known as Stormyr This area was taken over by *Carex filiformis* whose soft grey-green colour and waving slender

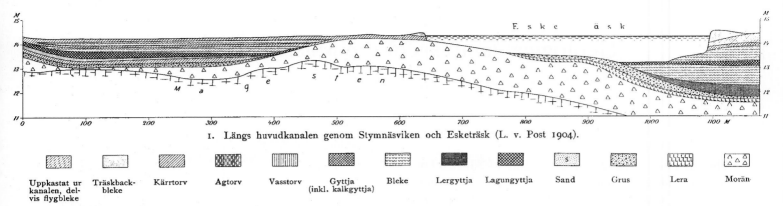

1. Längs huvudkanalen genom Stymnäsviken och Esketräsk (L. v. Post 1904).

Uppkastat ur kanalen, delvis flygbleke | Träskback-bleke | Kärrtorv | Agtorv | Vasstorv | Gyttja (inkl. kalkgyttja) | Bleke | Lergyttja | Lagungyttja | Sand | Grus | Lera | Morän

Fig. 1 Section through the Stymnäs inlet and Esketräsk, surveyed by L. von Post 1904. After von Post 1927 fig. 86:1 1) channel-upcast, partly windblown lake-marl, 2) fen bank marl, 3) peat, 4) *Cladium*-peat, 5) *Phragmites*-peat, 6) *gyttja*, 7) lake-marl, 8) clay—*gyttja* 9) lagoon—*gyttja*, 10) sand, 11) gravel, 12) clay 13) moraine.   Bedrock of marlstone (*märgelsten*).

leaves give an area a very different character from a covering of *Cladium*. *Phragmites* grew in a zone to the south-west and north/north-east of Nydträsk.

The vegetation was quite different in the northern parts of the fen, north-east of Storträsk and Risala träsk. Here the tussocky *Carex stricta* was predominant. Observations from similar sites elsewhere suggest that these large tussocks would often have served as the nesting sites for the birds of the fens.

The vegetation of the dryer marginal zones the *lagg* consisted of short *Carex* species, grasses and sedges (including *C panicea, C goudenoghii Schoenus* species and *Molinia* etc.)

The fen lakes

Bodies of water in the fen are of three types: shallow ponds (*vätar*) small pools (*punsar*) and swamps (*träsk*) The different types can usually if not always be distinguished.

The small shallow ponds (known locally as *vätar*) are only occasionally filled with water during periods of high water or after rain. The bottom is firm or covered by only a thin layer of lake marl. There is little plant life, but the lake marl is sometimes covered by a thin layer of algae (*myxophyceae*). This covering is important, as it prevents the fine marl from being blown away by the wind when the pond dries out. Large ponds of this type occur in the western part of the fen, south and north of Risala träsk.

The small pools (known locally as *punsar*) have peat bottoms and brown water Such pools usually occur in small groups especially north of Risala träsk and Storträsk and south-west of Nydträsk. Tunngans träsk is in

fact a pool of this type, but of exceptional size. The vegetation in these pools is minimal. The formation of the pools will be discussed below

The swamps are larger bodies of water characterised by lake marl and light (green) water Where the bottom is at a higher level it sometimes consists of moraine, sand or similar firm soil types From east to west the swamps are Nydträsk, Storträsk, Risala träsk and Eske träsk. The tool-chest was found in the area between the last two. The levels of the firm swamp bottom indicate that they were originally dammed up by ridges. The height above sea-level diminishes towards the west, Nydträsk being 14.8 m, Storträsk 14.6 m, Risala träsk 14.4 m and Eske träsk 14.3 m above sea level.

The banks of the swamps featured both erosion and accumulation. The narrow and relatively high ridges which occur with few exceptions on the west banks i.e. down-stream, are, however significant, and their origin will be discussed below The vegetation is usually insignificant, consisting mainly of sparse communities of *Phragmites* particularly along the western banks. There is sometimes a small amount of *Cladium*, as in Risala träsk.

The water table

The character of the fen is largely dependent on the water table. Travellers to Gotland will know it as an exceptionally dry area. Lakes are rare and those which do occur are shallow and very different from those on the mainland. Streams are also rare, being only shallow channels with dry stone bottoms. The reason for these differences is that the fluctuations in the water-level in Gotland are different from those on the mainland. In Gotland high water occurs in the winter· the water table

Fig. 2. Mästermyr with receding high water In the background Nydträsk. Photo L. von Post 1905. After von Post 1925 fig. 46.

beings to rise in the autumn as the result of persistent rains and continues to rise until it begins to fall again in the spring. The water table is lowest in the summer This explains one of the characteristic features of the fens and ponds. During the season when the watercourses are in flood, the fens, ponds and hollows are also filled with water and the streams cannot cut a channel trough them. The streams are therefore divided into short sections which come to an end every time they reach a hollow in the ground.

In the past this was the case at Mästermyr In the north the winding Levide stream abruptly stopped as it reached the fen *lagg* west–south–west of Tungelbos. To the south–east of Sproge chruch two small streams merged with the shallow fen. In the east was the Oxarve stream (also known as *Stångå*). von Post (1927) studied the mouth of this stream, which he saw as a typical example of a Gotland stream. The deposition of sediment was highest near the mouth of the stream, becoming successively lower further away· these features have now been obliterated by cultivation. Detailed measurements of the sediment cone of the Oxarve stream showed two marks, or 'floors' as von Post calls them (1927 p. 114), which correspond to the two main water-levels, high-water and low-water Both were marked as more or less sharply defined notches in the bank.

While the high-water level persisted the water which was carried to the fen spread evenly over the entire area, but it was nontheless possible to establish that it collected in certain channels. The most important of these was in the north, where the fen was at a slightly lower level. A weak run-off emanated from Hemd-arveviken in this area. Ljungqvist (1914, p. 2) observed

that the largest channels flow through *Carex stricta* communities. This was the case at *Stapler* a small area of *lagg* 1.5 km south–east of Sallmunds. This flow continued to Storträsk from which *Storränneln* leads to Risala träsk. At the west bank of this swamp the flow of the stream had increased and continued gaining strength to the outfall at Stenbro bridge. The watercourses suggested by Ljungqvist seem broadly correct, although the primary evidence appears to be a little weak. However it is unfortunately not possible to verify his conclusions today

It is evident, however that there was a distinct run off of water from east to west. When the ice broke up the floes would follow the same current, pushing more or less strongly westwards The effect can still be seen today because the west banks of the swamps have been pushed up into ridges by the thrust of the ice. A ridge of this type has been found on the east bank in only one case, at Storträsk, where a ridge occurs inside the long spit *Storsäv* This shore structure, the remains of which can still be seen, was formed at the end of the last century

Another effect of the water run-off, probably coupled with the ice, was the formation of the groups of small pools. Their proximity in certain parts of the fen seems very strange. von Post (1927 p. 110) associated their origin with the set of the current: one cannot doubt that one of the main causes of the formation of the pool groups and of Tunngans was the set of the current during high-water periods which, when at its strongest, weakened soil formation and held back the fen vegetation to allow bare patches of open water to appear It is likely that ice floes with sharp corners thrown about in such places could easily have damaged the peat cover

Fig. 3 Wind drift of lake marl in the main channel of Mästermyr in the summer of 1922. Photo C. Samuelsson. After von Post 1927 fig. 83

and made way for renewed attacks from frost and other damaging phenomena.

The evolution of the fen

Having established the general appearance of Mästermyr before it was drained, the history of its development can be traced on the basis of some of von Post's sections (1927 Fig. 86) These show a sequence of peat (including fen peat, *Cladium* peat etc.) on top of lake marl or calcareous *gyttja*, marine *gyttja* or clay *gyttja* in various combinations but always with clay *gyttja* at the bottom (see Fig. 1). According to von Post (1927 p. 120) the 'Mäster lake of the Ancylus and early Littorina stages probably did not extend west of the Eske träsk area, while large portions of the remaining area lay above water level. During the Littorina stage radical changes took place in the area when an arm of the Baltic reached across the present fenlands. The massive raised beach ridge at Snoder was formed at this time (von Post 1903 and Lundqvist 1965) the main road runs on top of and alongside this ridge today This is in fact a double ridge, corresponding to two layers of marine *gyttja* in the fen. Biologically they are characterised by the presence of *Cardium, Tellina* and other salt water molluscs. A layer of lake marl between the two marine strata (von Post 1927 Fig. 86:2–3) indicates that the fen lay above sea level for a short period but was subsequently submerged again. Whether this was due to a movement in the earth s crust or to changes in the sea level will not be discussed here.

When the land had finally risen above sea level, a marl swamp developed of approximately the same type as Storträsk before it was drained, although of much larger dimensions.

This large 'Mäster swamp gradually filled up, although not completely The vegetation consisted of sedges, reeds and other plants typical of the Gotland fens. We have no detailed information as to the extent of the plant cover and its constituents. However it can be deduced from the structure of the peat that the fen basin reacted with some sensitivity to the post-arctic climatic changes. The peat contains highly-decayed layers probably produced by *parvocariceta* i.e. sedge communities which prefer a dryer habitat of the fen *lagg* type. Small sedge species and rush grasses like *Carex glauca, C panices C flava* and *Schoenus* species etc. were probably important constituents. Evidence from pollen analysis suggests that the dryer stages of the development of the fen occurred at the end of the early Iron Age and again some time before the Viking Age. However it must be emphasised that pollen analysis diagrams from Gotland are difficult to interpret because of the erratic nature of the strata. Zones which represent a long period of time may be extremely compressed and others extended. Such apparently erratic stratification is typical of shallow basins in areas of relatively low precipitation.

The summarised results of existing pollen analysis diagrams seem to indicate that the dryer periods were of relatively short duration, and were followed by a fairly rapid return to the conditions which existed before, probably because the whole of the area of fenland did not reach the dry stage. The typical fenland vegetation had probably remained in waterlogged hollows and swamps from which it could quickly extend over the fen when this again received a sufficient flow of water

The Viking Age fen

The above account considers the appearance of the fen before draining and the general lines of its post-arctic evolution. It remains to establish the conditions in the area at the time from which the tool-chest dates. We are fortunate to have a section drawn by von Post in 1904 (Fig. 1) from an area very close to the site of the find to the east of Eske träsk. The section shows that the layers of peat are very much reduced, which means that sedimentation was well advanced before the filling-in with vegetation began. The strata cannot be dated any more closely on the site, but some indications can be deduced from the sequence of strata elsewhere in the fen which have been dated by pollen analysis. It would seem that the water table in the fen was relatively high in the Viking Age. The ridges along the swamp banks already existed and were still growing. We do not know how far the ridge east of Eske träsk had developed, but on the available evidence elsewhere, one may hazard a guess that it was almost complete at this time. Although the material is not as complete as one would wish, the results of the present study indicate that during the Viking Age the fen looked very much as it did before it was drained in 1902.

Appendix II
Metallographic examination of some iron objects from Mästermyr
by Sten Modin

It is generally believed that early iron production in Sweden was based on lake or bog ore. The iron was extracted from the ore with the aid of charcoal in small low furnaces. The bloom produced in these furnaces was of a very heterogeneous composition, the carbon content in particular could vary considerably within the same piece.

This paper is based on an investigation made in 1953 Most studies carried out on iron finds at that time consisted of chemical analyses. microscopic examination of the structure was rare. Microscopic studies can yield information about the method of production, the homogeneous nature of the material and any heat treatment of the piece. It can be ascertained whether several pieces were welded together and whether the surface of the steel was carburised by cementation to increase its hardness, etc.

The following objects were examined. sledge hammer no. 69, adze no. 64, axe no. 62, spoon-auger no. 48, saw no. 42 and trace ring no. 88 The objects date from the eleventh century [1]

It was desirable to cause as little damage as possible to the objects under examination. The usual procedure—removing test pieces by sawing or drilling—could therefore not be employed. Therefore a test area, not exceeding one square centimetre, was selected on each object. The surface was there filed down to remove the rust, producing a flat area which was then ground on emery paper polished and etched. [2] Because of the size and shape of the objects the resulting test areas were not as satisfactory as if normal test pieces had been prepared.

Spoon-auger no 48   Fig. 1–3

The test area included the cutting edge and its immediate surrounds. Two materials of different carbon contents were observed. The dividing line was fairly sharp and marked by a slag zone. One material forms the actual edge: its carbon content is about 0.4 % and it has a martensitic structure; the other material, in the shank, has a very low carbon content of about 0.02 % and is therefore almost pure iron. The slag zone consists of silica-type grains. There are no sulphide inclusions

It is clear that the material at the edge, with its higher carbon content, was welded to the softer material in the shank. The slag zone seems mainly to be produced by the fluxing agent, probably sand, which was used in the welding. The martensitic structure of the carbon-rich edge shows that the tool was finally heated and quenched.

Sledge hammer no 69   Fig. 4–6

The test area was on the peen of the sledge hammer At least two materials with different carbon contents were observed. The dividing line was continuous and not marked by a slag zone. The material at the far end of the peen has the higher carbon content, about 0.4 %, and a martensitic structure. The other softer material lies further from the end and has a carbon content of about 0.05 %. The slag, abundant in some places is of silica type. There are no sulphide inclusions.

The material with higher carbon content at the end of the peen seems to be welded to the softer material and not carburised by cementation. The sledge hammer was forged at high temperatures which caused some of the carbon in the harder material to transfer to the softer material and create a diffuse border area. Finally the tool was heated and quenched.

Adze no 64   Fig. 7

The test area was part of the cutting edge of the adze. The edge is of hardened steel with a carbon content of about 0.4 %. A light streak with accompanying slag zone, parallel to the blade of the adze, suggests that it was welded together from two pieces of steel with approximately the same carbon content. Slag inclusions are of the silica type and there are no sulphide inclusions.

See chapter 5.

[2] In all cases the etching was done in 1 % nitric acid in alcohol.

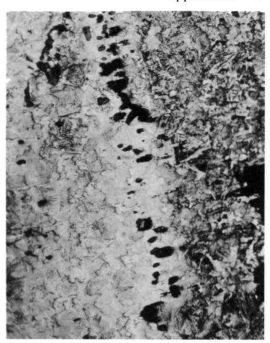

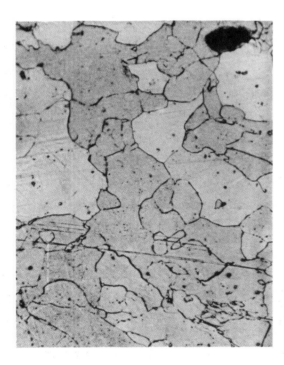

Spoon auger no. 48.
Fig. 1 Martensitic structure at the edge. 200×
Fig. 2. Transitional zone between the hard material at the edge and the soft material of the shank. The zone is marked by a line of slag. 200×
Fig. 3. The soft material of the shank is almost pure iron. A slag inclusion of silica-type. 200×

and runs parallel to the blade of the axe. The soft material has abundant round and relatively large silica inclusions and occasional iron sulphide inclusions, which may indicate that this material is brittle at red-heat. The steel fractured when the blade was bent. The reason for the bending of the axe blade is not known.

Trace-ring no 88   Fig. 9

The test area was situated on the surface of the ring. It consists of virtually carbon-free iron, with only occasional iron carbide at the grain boundaries Inside the iron grains, rod-like formations reminiscent of iron nitride, are precipitated. Iron nitride may have been formed by strong blasts of air during iron smelting. Slag inclusions are of silica type and occur rather sparingly considering the low carbon content of the material. No sulphide inclusions were observed.

Axe no. 62   Fig. 8

A section situated where the blade of the axe had been bent over was tested. Two materials with different carbon content were observed, one with a carbon content of about 0.4 % and a hardening structure, the other with a slightly unevenly distributed carbon content averaging 0.05 %. The dividing line between the two is sharp

Sledge hammer no. 69.
Fig. 4. Martensitic structure at the end of the peen. 150×
Fig. 5. Transitional zone between the soft and the hard material. 150×
Fig. 6. A large slag inclusion at the transitional zone between soft and hard material. 150×

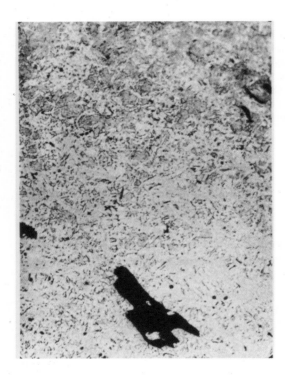

The saw no. 42

One area of a saw-tooth was examined, showing that it consisted of virtually carbon-free iron. Iron carbide occurred occasionally at the grain boundaries. No traces at all could be found of carburising of the surface. If such carburising occurred, it must have been extremely weak and have rusted away Considering the iron s low carbon content, and resulting softness the tool must have rapidly become worn during use. Slag inclusions are of silicon type, and are relatively few considering the low carbon content of the material. No sulphide inclusions have been traced.

Conclusions

The investigation shows that the objects were made from fairly homogeneous iron pieces. Pieces of different carbon content were often welded together if required and forged to the desired shape. Processes of hardening by heat treatment were known and were carried out to improve the performance of the tools. With one exception there were no sulphide inclusions and the sulphur content is therefore low Slag inclusions are usually of silica type. The objects were made at a time and place where the methods of producing and working iron were highly developed.

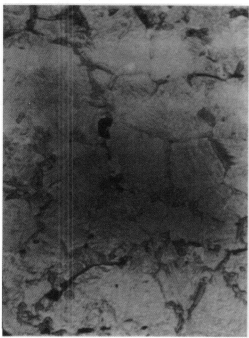

Adze no. 64.
Fig. 7 Martensitic structure at the edge.
Dark slag inclusions. 150x.

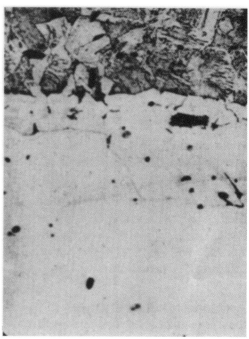

Axe no. 62.
Fig. 8. Transitional zone between hard and
soft material. 150x.

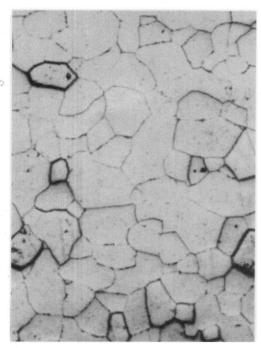

Trace-ring no. 88.
Fig. 9. Structure of the ring. 150x

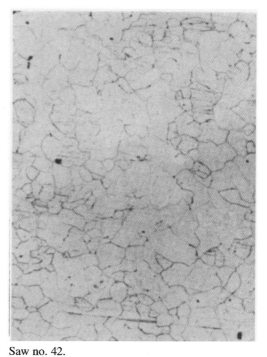

Saw no. 42.
Fig. 10. Structure of a saw-teeth. 150x.

Appendix III

Professor Torsten Lagerberg's identifications of wood samples from the Mästermyr find are as follow·

The chest: the lid and sides are of oak.
Key no. 3· the handle is of ash.
Saw no. 42: the handle is of ash.
(?)Scribing tool no. 97·   the handle is of ash.
Tool no. 96: the handle is of spruce.
The worked pieces of wood nos. 129 and 130 are of maple.

According to this report, dated 26.11 1952, it seems that the three ash-wood handles were all fashioned from branches.

Abbreviations

ATA	Antikvarisk–Topografiska Arkivet, Stockholm
Gotl. F	Gotlands Fornsal, Visby
INAU	Institute of Northeuropean Archaeology at the University of Uppsala
IAUS	Institute of Archaeology at the University of Stockholm
KVHAA	Kungl. Vitterhets Historie och Antikvitets Akademien
MLHM	Meddelanden från Lunds Historiska Museum
MS	Unpublished manuscript
SGU	Sveriges Geologiska Undersökning
SHM	Statens Historiska Museum
VZG	Völkerwanderungszeit Gotlands. See Nerman 19

Bibliography

Almgren, B. 1942. "Thors märke" och himmelrikets nycklar *Uppland*. Uppsala.
1946. Om vagnåkarnas färder *Gotländskt arkiv* Visby
1955. Bronsnycklar och djurornamentik. *Diss* Uppsala.
Alvar M. 1948. El habla del Campo da Jaco. Salamanca.
Ambrosiani, B. (ed.), 1973. *See* Birka. Svarta jordens hamnområde.
Ambrosiani, S., 1913. Gammaldags logbelysning. *Fataburen*. Stockholm.
Andersen, H. H. Crabb, P J and Madsen, H. J 1971 Århus Søndervold—en byarkeologisk undersøgelse. København.
Anderson, J 1881 Scotland in Early Christian Times. Edinburgh.
Anker P & Topelius, A.-S., 1963. Kister *Kulturhistoriskt lexikon för nordisk medeltid* 8. Malmö.
Arbman, H., 1937 En 1000-årig verktygslåda. *Metallarbetaren* 35. Stockholm.
1940. Der Årby-Fund. *Acta Archaeologica* 9. København.
1940, 1943. *See* Birka 1
1963. Jönköpingstrakten under förhistorisk tid. *Jönköpings stads historia* 1 Värnamo.
Arbman, H. & Nilsson, N.-O. 1969. Armes scandinaves de l'époque Viking en France. *MLHM* 66–68. Lund.
Arrhenius, B. 1976. Die ältesten Funde von Birka. *Prähistorische Zeitschrift* 51:2. Berlin.
Arwidsson, G., 1942. Valsgärde 6. Uppsala. *Die Gräberfunde von Valsgärde* 1 Uppsala.
1954. Valsgärde 8. *Die Gräberfunde von Valsgärde* 2. Uppsala.
1977 Valsgärde 7 *Die Gräberfunde von Valsgärde* 3. Uppsala.
Beck, L., 1884. Die Geschichte des Eisens in technischer und kulturgeschichtlicher Beziehung. Braunschweig.
1902. Der Einfluss der römischen Herrschaft auf die deutsche Industri. *Festschrift des Germanisch-Römisches Zentralmuseums* Mainz.
Behrens, G., 1939. Merowingische Gewichte und Waagen. *Mainzer Zeitschrift* 34. Mainz.
Bencard, M. 1979. Wikingerzeitliches Handwerk in Ribe. *Acta Archaeologica* 49. København.
Bender Jørgensen, H. & Skov T., 1980. Trabjerg. *Acta Archaeologica* 50. København.
Bengtsson, B., 1945. Äldre guldsmedsteknik *Svenskt silversmide 1520–1850* 3. Stockholm.
1973. Redskap och symbol. Något om guldsmedens boraxfass. *Kulturen Årsbok*. Lund.
Berg, A. Christensen jr A. E. & Liestøl, A. 1966. Lås. *Kulturhistoriskt lexikon för nordisk medeltid* 11 Malmö.
Berg, G. 1955. A Tool Chest from the Viking Age (the Mästermyr Find in Gotland). A preliminary account. *Universitetet i Bergen*. *Årbok*. Historisk–antikvarisk rekke 1 Bergen.
1958. The Sawing by Hand of Boards and Planks. *Folk-Liv* 1957–58. Stockholm.

Bergens museums årbok. 1913 nr 13. Tillvekst 1912. Bergen.
Beskow-Sjöberg, M., 1977 The Archaeology of Skedemosse 4. *KVHAA Monographien* 57 Stockholm.
Birka 1 Untersuchungen und Studien publ. by *KVHAA* 1940, 1943 Stockholm.
Birka. Svarta jordens hamnområde. Riksantikvarieämbetet. Rapport C 1 1973. Stockholm.
Blindheim, Ch. 1963. Smedgraven fra Bygland i Morgedal. *Viking* Oslo.
Blomqvist, R. 1940. Medeltida bultlås och bultlåsnycklar från Lund. *Kulturen. Årsbok*. Lund.
Bohlin, P.-O. 1981 Brakteatteknik. *MS* IANU
Bomann, W 1929. Bäuerliches Hauswesen und Tagewerk im alten Niedersachsen. 2nd ed. Weimar
Bourke, C. 1980, Early Irish Hand-Bells. *Journal of the R Society of Antiquaries of Ireland* 110. Dublin.
Boye, V 1858. To fund af smedsvaerktöi fra den siste hedniske tid i Danmark. *Annaler for nordisk oldkyndighed* København.
Brate, E. & Wessén, E. 1924–1936. Södermanlands runinskrifter. *KVHAA Monographien*. Stockholm.
Bringéus, N.-A. 1958. Klockringningsseden i Sverige. *Diss* Stockholm.
Bruce-Mitford, R. 1972. The Sutton Hoo Ship-Burial. London.
Bruckner A. o.a. (eds.), 1939. Encyklopedia staropolska. Warszawa.
Brøndsted, J 1936. Danish Inhumation Graves of the Viking Age. *Acta Archaeologica* 7 København.
1960, 1966. Danmarks Oldtid 3. Jernalderen. 2nd and 3rd ed. København.
Böhner K. 1939. Ein fränkischer Goldschmiedgrab aus dem Neuwieder Becken. *Rheinische Vorzeit in Wort und Bild*. 2–3. Düsseldorf.
Calissendorff, K. 1979. Linguistic Evidence for Early Iron Production. *Iron and Man in Prehistoric Sweden*. Stockholm.
Campbell, Å. 1950. Det svenska brödet. En jämförande etnologisk undersökning. Stockholm.
Carlsson, S. J 1958. Anteckningar om Ulrika socken. Linköping.
Collin-Schlyter (ed.), 1834. Upplands-Lagen. Stockholm.
Crabb, P J 1971 *See* Andersen.
Cruden, S. 1965. Excavations at Birsay Orkney *The Fourth Viking Congress* August 1961 York.
Cursiter J W 1856. Notice of a Wood-Carvers Tool-Box *Proceedings of the Society of Antiquaries of Scotland* 20. Edinburgh.
Darnay K. 1906. Restes d'une usine celtique et de fonderies. *Archeologia Ertesitö* 26. Budapesti.
Déchelette, J 1903. *See* Pagés-Allary
1914. Manuel d'archeologie préhistorique, Celtique et Gallo-Romaine. 2. Paris.
1927 Manuel d'archeologie celtique 4. Paris.
Dehn, W 1976. Bibracte. *Reallexikon der Germanischen*

52 Bibliography

Altertumskunde 2. Berlin.

Delbrueck, R. 1929. Die Consulardiptychen und verwandte Denkmäler *Studien zur spätantike Kunstgeschichte* 2. Berlin.

Ekholm, G. 1939. Valloxsäby kvarnbacke. *Fornvännen.* Stockholm.

1944. Uppländska gravfält från äldre järnålder *Fornvännen.* Stockholm.

Engelhardt, C. 1869. Fynske Mosefund 2. Vimose Fundet. København.

Engelstad, E. 1944. De eldste norske kistene. *Viking* 8. Oslo.

Erixon, S. 1947 Låset förr och nu. Ur låsets utvecklingshistoria. *På järnets fasta grund.* Eskilstuna.

Espérandieu, E. 1907–1928. Recueil général des bas-reliefs, statues et bustes de la Gaule romaine. Paris.

Etnografia Shqiptare 1 1962. Tirana.

Excavations at Helgö 5:1 1978. *KVHAA* Stockholm.

Falk, H. 1912. Altnordisches Seewesen. *Wörter und Sachen* 4. Heidelberg.

Filip, J. 1956. Die Kelten in Mitteleuropa. Praha.

1966. Enzyklopädisches Handbuch zur Ur- und Frühgeschichte Europas. Prag.

Frost, G. 1941 Järnarbete. *Skansvakten* 26. Mora.

Fynd och fältarbeten, 1937 Tillfällig utställning. Statens historiska museum och Riksantikvarieämbetet. Stockholm.

Gaitzsch, W 1978. Römische Werkzeuge. *Kleine Schriften zur Kenntnis der römischen Besetzungsgeschichte Südwestdeutschlands*

1980. Eiserne Werkzeuge 1–2. *British Archaeological Reports International Series* 78:11 Oxford.

Gaitzsch W & Matthäus, H., 1980. Schreinerwerkzeuge aus dem Kastell Altstadt. *Archäologisches Korrespondenzblatt* 10. Mainz.

Gejvall, N.-G. 1948. *See* Sahlström.

Gauchet, L. 1909. Les noms romanes de la chlochettes de vaches. *Bulletin du Glossaire* 8. Paris.

Goodman, W L. 1964. The History of Woodworking Tools. London.

Granlund, J., 1944. Avlöningsformer *Arbetaren i helg och söcken. Den svenska arbetarklassens historia.* Stockholm.

Grieg, S. 1920–22. Smedeverktøi i norske gravfund. *Oldtiden* 9. Oslo.

1928. Osebergfundet 2. Oslo.

1938. Tromsø museums oldsaksamling 1923. *Tromsø Museums årshefte* 47 Tromsø.

Gräslund, A-S. 1980. The Burial Customs. *Diss* Uppsala. = *Birka. Untersuchungen und Studien.* 4. *KVHAA Monographien.* Stockholm.

Grøn, F 1927 Om kostholdet i Norge indtil aar 1500. Oslo.

Gustavson, H. 1938. Gotlands ortnamn. En översikt. *Ortnamnssällskapets i Uppsala årsskrift* Uppsala.

Hagar H. 1970. Seldon. *Kulturhistoriskt lexikon för nordisk medeltid* 15. Malmö.

1973. Die Zugvorrichtungen bei dem zweispännigen Ackerwagen für Pferde in Skandinavien und Finnland. *Land Transport in Europe Studies of Folklife* 4. Copenhagen.

Hagberg, U E. 1967 The Archaeology of Skedemosse 1–2. *KVHAA Monographien* 46. Stockholm.

Hallinder P 1978. Currency bars of Mästermyr type. *Excavations at Helgö* 5:1 KVHAA, Stockholm.

Hanssen, B. 1952. Österlen. *Diss* Stockholm.

Hauck, K. 1977 Wielands Hort. Die sozialgeschichtliche Stellung des Schmiedes in frühen Bildprogrammen nach und vor dem Religionswechsel. *Antikvariskt Arkiv* 64. KVHAA. Stockholm,

Hellner B. 1948. Järnsmidet i Vasatidens dekorativa konst. *Diss* Stockholm.

Hellner B. & Rooth, S. 1960. Konstsmide. Historia och teknik. Stockholm.

Heyerdahl-Larsen, E. 1979–80. Kobberkjelen i Gokstadskipet. *Sandefjordmuseerne Årbok.* Sandefjord.

Holmgren, G 1933. Gravfältet på Mora äng. *Uppsala Nya Tidnings julnummer* Uppsala.

Holmquist, W 1979. Sweden's First Industrial Society *Iron and Man in Prehistoric Sweden.* Stockholm.

Homman, O. 1941 Kista från Lillhärdal. *Fataburen.* Stockholm.

1966. Lås. Sverige. *Kulturhistoriskt lexikon för nordisk medeltid* 11 Malmö.

Hvass, S. 1979. Die Völkerwanderungzeitliche Siedlung Vorbasse, Mitteljütland. *Acta Archaelogica* 49. København.

1980. Vorbasse. The Viking-age Settlement at Vorbasse. *Acta Archaeologica* 50. København.

Hårdh, B. 1976 A. Wikingerzeitliche Depotfunde aus Südschweden. *Diss* Lund.

1976 B. Wikingerzeitliche Depotfunde aus Südschweden. Katalog und Tafeln. *Acta Archaeologica Lundensia.* Series in 4° No 9. Lund.

Jacobi G 1974. Werkzeug und Gerät aus dem Oppidum von Manching. *Die Ausgrabungen in Manching* 5. Wiesbaden.

Jankuhn, H., 1972. Haithabu, ein Handelsplatz der Wikingerzeit. Neumünster

Jansson, S. O. 1936. Mått, mål och vikt till 1500-talets mitt. *Nordisk Kultur* 30. Stockholm.

1945. Besmanet i förhållande till andra olikartade vågar *MS*

1982. Besman och Doltje. Tvärvetenskapligt försök. *Tal om blandade ämnen. Collegium curiosorum novum* 2. Uppsala.

Jernkontorets Annaler 1845. Stockholm.

Joensen, J P 1980. Färöisk folkkultur Lund.

Joffroy R. 1960. L oppidum de Vix et la civilisation Hallstattien finale dans l'est de la France. *Diss* Paris.

Kaland, S. H. H. 1969. Studier i Øvre Telemarks vikingtid. *Universitetets Oldsaksamling Årbok.* Oslo.

Karlson, W 1928, Studier i Sveriges medeltida möbelkonst. Diss. Lund

Keyland, N 1919. Svensk allmogekost. 1 Vegetabilisk allmogekost. Stockholm.

Kisa, A. 1908. Das Glas im Altertume. 1–3. Leipzig.

Klindt-Jensen, O. 1953 Bronzekedelen fra Brå. *Jysk arkeologisk Selskabs Skrifter* 3. Aarhus.

1957 Bornholm i folkvanderingstid. *Nationalmuseets skrifter* 2. København.

1978. Slusegårdgravpladsen 1–2. *Jysk arkeologisk Selskabs skrifter* 14:2. Aarhus.

Klintberg, M. Anteckningar N:ris 62 efter smeden S. L. Lyander i Lau, född 1821 *MS* Sällskapet för gotländsk forskning. Landsarkivet. Visby

Klintberg, M. & Gustavson, H. 1972–1982. *See* Ordbok.

Klumbach, H. 1973 Der römische Skulpturfund von Hausen an der Zaber (Kr Heilbronn) *Forschungen und Berichte zur Vor- und Frühgeschichte in Baden-Würtemberg* 5. Stuttgart.

Kolčin, B. A. 1959. *See* Trucy Novgoroskoj ekspedicii.

Krogh, K. J & Voss, O., 1961 Fra hedenskab til kristendom. *Fra Nationalmuseets Arbejdsmark.* København.

Krüger F 1939. Die Hochpyrenäen C 2. Hamburg.

Lamm, J P 1962. Ett medeltida gravfynd från Spelvik. *Fornvännen.* Stockholm.

Lauby A. 1903 *See* Pagés-Allary

Leppäaho, J. 1949. Räisälän Hovinsaarin Tontinmäen paja, sen langanvetovälineet ja langanvedosta (vanutuksesta) yleensäkin. *Suomen Museo* 56. Helsinki.
1951. Napakaira 1 *Kalevalaseuran Vuosikirja* 31 Helsinki.

Liestøl, A. 1976. Øks. *Kulturhistoriskt lexikon för nordisk medeltid* 20. Malmö.

Lima och Transtrand, 1982. Ur två socknars historia 1 Malung.

Lindberg, F 1947 Hantverkarna 1 *Den svenska arbetarklassens historia.* Stockholm.

Lindenschmit, L. 1911 Altertümer unserer heidnischen Vorzeit. 5. Mainz.

Lindqvist, S. 1914. Ramsundsbron vid Sigurdristningen och en storbondesläkt från missionstiden. *Fornvännen.* Stockholm.
1936. Gamla Uppsala och Ottarshögen. KVHAA *Monographien* 23. Stockholm.
1941–1942. Gotlands Bildsteine 1–2. *KVHAA Monographien* 29. Stockholm.

Lithberg, N 1914. Koskällan. *Fataburen.* Stockholm.

Ljunggren, K. G., 1965. Landebokens tillkomst och innehåll. Lund.

Ljungqvist, J. E., 1906. En gotländsk myr Svenska Turistföreningens årsskrift. Stockholm.
1914. Mästermyr En växtekologisk studie. *Diss* Uppsala.

Lundqvist, G. 1927 Myrmarker *Beskrivning till kartbladet Klintehamn. SGU Aa No 160.* Stockholm.
1965. C 14-dateringar från Gotland. SGU C No 602. Stockholm.

Madsen, H. I. 1971 *See* Andersen.

Magnusson, G. 1978. Järnhanteringen i Jämtland och Härjedalen. En presentation av forskningsuppgifter *Jernkontorets forskningsserie H* No 17 Stockholm.

Manninen, I. 1933. Die Sachkultur Estlands 2. Tartu.

Matsson, N H., 1953. Brassa bjällror *Skinnarbygd* 6. Malung.

Merving, W 1958. (Report). *Fornvännen.* Stockholm.

Miclea, J 1980. Geto—Dacii. Bukaresti.

von Miske, K. 1908. Die praehistorische Ansiedlung Velim St. Vid. Wien.

Moberg, C-A. 1955. Studier i bottnisk stenålder *KVHAA Handlingar* 3. Stockholm.

Modin, S. & Pleiner S. 1978. The metallographic examinations of locks, keys and tools. *Excavations at Helgö* 5:1 Workshop 2. KVHAA. Stockholm.

Moszyński, K. 1929. Kultura ludowa słovian 1 Kraków.

Munthe, H. Hede, J E. och von Post. L. 1927 Beskrivning till kartbladet Hemse. SGU Aa No 164. Stockholm.

Müller-Wille, M. 1977 Der frühmittelalterliche Schmied im Spiegel Skandinavischer Grabfunde. *Frühmittelalterliche Studien.* Band 11 Berlin.

Mårtensson, A. W' 1972. Medeltida metallhantverk i Lund. *Kulturen. Årsbok.* Lund.

1976. Uppgrävt förflutet för PKbanken i Lund. En investering i arkeologi. *Archaeologica Lundensia* 7 Lund.

Møhl, U 1968. Knoglematerialet fra Pedersstraede i Viborg. *Kuml.* Århus.

Möllerheim, J MS in Science of Gunnery Handbok. Armémuseum. Stockholm.

Möllerop, O. 1961 Foreløpig meddelelse om et smedgravfunn fra Vestly i Time. *Stavanger Museum. Årbok.* Stavanger

Nerman, B. 1935. Die Völkerwanderungszeit Gotlands. *KVHAA Monographien* 21 Stockholm.

Neubert, G. S. 1969. Skandinaviske jernklokker til husdyr set i europeisk sammenhang. En historisk og geografisk undersøgelse. *MS* Nordiska Museet, Stockholm.

Nicolaissen, O. 1924. Arkeologiske undersökelser og tilveksten i Tromsö Museums oldsaksamling 1923 *Tromsö Museum. Årshefte 47* Tromsö.

N/ilsson/ H. 1941 Skällor *Kulturen. Årsbok.* Lund.

Noll, R. 1980. Das Inventar des Dolochenusheiligtums von Mauer an der Url (Noricum). (= Der römische Limes in Österreich, 30) Wien.

Nylén, E. 1955. Die jüngere vorrömische Eisenzeit Gotlands. *Diss* Uppsala.
1977 La Tèneproblemet—en nyckelfråga. *Fornvännen.*

Ohlhaver H. 1939. Der germanische Schmied und sein Werkzeug. Leipzig.

Olaus Magnus, 1555. Historia de gentibus septentrionalibus. Roma.

Oldeberg, A. 1966. Metallteknik under vikingatid och medeltid. Stockholm.

Olsen, O. and Crumlin-Pedersen, O. 1967 The Skuldelev Ships 2. *Acta Archaeologica* 38. København.

Ordbok över Laumålet på Gotland. På grundval av Mathias Klintbergs samlingar utarbetad av Herbert Gustavson, 1:1972– Uppsala.

Pagés-Allary J Déchelette, J & Lauby A. 1903. Le Tumulus Arverne de Celles pres Neussarques (Cantal). Auvergne. *L Antropologie* 14. Paris.

Paret, O. 1939. Von römischen Schnellwaagen und Gewichte. *Saalburg-Jahrbuch* 9. Frankfurt a. M.

Petersen, J 1919. De norske vikingesverd. Kristiania.
1951 Vikingetidens redskaper Oslo.

Pleiner R. 1962. Alteuropäisches Schmiedehandwerk. Stand der metallkundlichen Forschung. Prag.
1975. Eisenschmiede im frühmittelalterlichen Zentraleuropa. Die Wege zur Erforschung eines Handwerkszweiges. *Frühmittelalterliche Studien* 9. Berlin.

von Post, L. 1903. En profil genom högsta Litorinavallen på södra Gotland. *SGU C No 195* Stockholm.
1925. Myrar träsk och vätar *Gotlands geologi En översikt SGU C No 331* Stockholm.
1927 *Beskrivning till kartbladet Hemse SGU Aa No 164* Stockholm.

Press, B. 1974. Gotländska släkter och gårdar Visby

Påhlsson, I. 1977 A Standard Pollen Diagram from the Lojsta Area of Central Gotland. *Striae* 3. Uppsala.

Rudberg, E. 1952. Metallografiska institutets Forskningsverksamhet 3, Juli–December 1952. Stockholm.

Rydh H. 1936. Förhistoriska undersökningar på Adelsö. *KVHAA Monographien* 24. Stockholm.

Rygh, O. 1885. Norske oldsager Kristiania.

Rålamb, Å. C. 1644. Skeps Byggerij eller Adelig Öfnings tionde tom. Stockholm.

Sahlström, K. E., 1954. Bankälla och Stora Ro. Två västgötska brandgropsgravfält. *KVHAA Handlingar* 89. Stockholm.

Sahlström, K. E. & Gejvall, N-G 1948. Gravfältet på kyrkbacken i Horns socken, Västergötland. *KVHAA Handlingar* 60. Stockholm.

Sandklef, A. 1951 Några halländska torvmossefynd. *Varbergs Museum. Årsbok*. Varberg.

Sarauw G. & Alin, J 1923 Götaälvsområdets fornminnen. Göteborg.

von Schoultz, G. 1949. Kistor Stockholm.

Schmidt, B. 1976. Archäologische Forshungen zur Völkerwanderungszeit und zur fränkisch–karolingisch–frühdeutschen Zeit und zum hohen Mittelalter *Ausgrabungen und Funde* 21 Berlin.

Schubert, F & Hoerschelmann, S. 1978. Archäologie und Photographie, Mainz.

Schwab, H., 1972. Entdeckung einer keltischen Brücke an der Zihl und ihre Bedeutung für La Tène. *Archäologisches Korrespondenzblatt* 3. Mainz.

Sernander R. 1939. Linné och den sydsvenska granskogsgränsen. *Svenska Linné-sällskapets årsskrift* Uppsala.

Serning, I. 1966. Dalarnas järnålder *KVHAA Monographien* 45. Stockholm.
1973. Förhistorisk järnhantering i Dalarna. Fältundersökningar och tekniska undersökningar *Jernkontorets forskningsserie* H. No. 9. Stockholm.
1979 A. Prehistoric Iron Production. *Iron and Man in prehistoric Sweden*. Ed. *Helen Clarke* Stockholm.
1979 B. Malm, Metall, Föremål. *MS*, IAUS.

Silvia, T 1980. Das Werkzeugdepot von Lozna (Kr Botosani). *Dacia* 24. Bucaresti.

Simonsen, P., 1953. Smedgraven fra Ytre Elgsnes. *Viking* Oslo.

Sjøvold, Th. 1974. The Iron Age Settlement of Arctic Norway 2. *Tromsö Museums skrifter* 10:2. Oslo.

Singer Ch. (ed.), 1954. A History of Technology 1 Oxford.

Skjølsvold, A., 1969. En fangstmanns grav i Trysil-fjellene. *Viking* 33. Oslo.

Skov T 1980. *See* Bender Jørgensen.

Smith, Ch. R. 1861 Collectanea antiqua 5. London.

Sovietskaja Etnografija 1953 (Report), Moskva.

Stenberger M., 1933. Öland under äldre järnålder *Diss KVHAA Monographien* 19. Stockholm.
1935. Gravfältet vid Gannor i Lau. *Gotländskt Arkiv* Visby.
1947 & 1958. Die Schatzfunde Gotlands der Wikingerzeit 1–2. *KVHAA Monographien* 34. Stockholm.
1955. Vallhagar A Migration Period Settlement on Gotland, Sweden. 1–2. Ed. M. Stenberger Copenhagen.
1961 Das Gräberfeld bei Ihre im Kirchspiel Hellvi auf Gotland. *Acta Archaeologica* 32. København.

Stenton, F., 1958. The Bayeux Tapestry London.

Stolpe, Hj. & Arne, T J 1912. Gravfältet vid Vendel. *KVHAA Monographien* 13. Stockholm.

Stoumann, J 1980. Sædding. A viking-age Village near Esbjerg. *Acta Archaeologica* 50. København.

Strömberg, M. 1961 Untersuchungen zur jüngeren Eisenzeit in Schonen. *Diss*. Lund.

Sundquist, N. 1934. En upländsk träkistgrav från vikingatiden. *Studier tillägnade G. Ekholm*. Uppsala.

Sundström, J., 1982. En skicklig hantverkare begravdes vid Drocksjön. *Historiska Nyheter* Statens historiska museum, No. 21 Stockholm.

Sveriges Natur 1924. *Svenska Naturskyddsföreningens årsskrift* Stockholm.

Swoboda, E. 1958. Carnuntum. Seine Geschichte und seine Denkmäler *Römische Forschungen in Niederösterreich* 1 Graz.

Sylvan, C. 1892. Gotlands naturbeskaffenhet. *Svenska Mosskulturföreningens Tidskrift*. Jönköping.

Szabó, M. 1971 Sur les traces des Celtes en Hongrie. Budapest.

Tegnér G 1973. Redskap från nyare tid i Statens historiska museums samlingar *Fornvännen*. Stockholm.

Teophilus, 1933. Diversarum artium schedula. Ed. W Theobald. Berlin.

Thunmark, L. 1974. Stämplar på gotländskt vikingasilver *Gotländskt Arkiv* Visby
1979. Burget på Burge—en storgård på gränsen mellan heden och kristen tid. *Arkeologi på Gotland. Visby.*

Thålin-Bergman, L. 1976. Øks. Sverige och Skåne. *Kulturhistoriskt lexikon för nordisk medeltid* 20. Malmö.
1979. Blacksmithing in Prehistoric Sweden. *Iron and Man in prehistoric Sweden*. Ed. *Helen Clarke* Stockholm.

Tobiassen, A, H. 1981 Smeden i eldre tid. Oslo.

Tomtlund, J-E., 1978 A. Locks and keys. *Excavations at Helgö*. 5:1 KVHAA. Stockholm.
1978 B Tools. *Excavations at Helgö* 5:1 Stockholm.

Trotzig, D. 1938. Laggningen på Sollerön, *Gruddbo på Sollerön. En byundersökning* Stockholm.

Trotzig, G 1972. En stavkyrka i Silte. *Gotländskt Arkiv* Visby
1978. Metallkärl av koppar och dess legeringar under vikingatid och tidig medeltid en systematisering. *Fornvännen*. Stockholm.

Trudy Novgoroskoj ekspedicii II. Ed. Arcichovskij A. V & Kolčin, B. A. 1959. *Materialy i issledovanija po archeologii SSSR* 65. Moskva.

van Tyghem, F 1966. Op en om de Middeleeuwse Bouwwerf. 1 Brussel.

Universitetets Oldsaksamlings tilvækst 1973–76, 1979. Oslo.

Uppgrävt förflutet, 1976. *Archaeologica Lundensia* 7 (See Mårtensson 1976).

Waagepetersen, Chr 1965. Forsvundne Tømmerøkser Et forsøg på en undersøgelse af redskaberne til en glemt håndværksteknik. Kalundborg,

Wagner F 1958. Denkmäler und Fundstätten der Vorzeit. München.

Wallander A. 1979. Smedgravar eller gravar med smides-och snickarverktyg? *MS* INAU

Valonen, N 1951 Napakaira 2. *Kalevalaseuran Vuosikirja* 31 Helsinki.

Werner J 1954. Waage und Geld in der Merowingerzeit. *Sitzungsbericht der Bayrischen Akademie der Wissenschaften*. München.

Vouga, B. 1923. La Tène. Leipzig.

Violant i Simorra, B. 1948. Art popular decoratiu. Barcelona.

Zachrisson, I. 1960. De ovala spännbucklornas tillverkningssätt, *Tor* Uppsala.
1962. Smedsfyndet från Smiss. *Tor* Uppsala.

Zachrisson, S. 1958. Några gravkistor av trä från tidig medeltid. *Tor* Uppsala.

Zelenin, D. 1927 Russische (Ostslavische) Volkskunde. Berlin.

Zeitler R. 1977–78. Om de medeltida landskyrkorna i Norden. *Kungl. humanistiska vetenskaps-samfundet i Uppsala. Årsbok*. Uppsala.

Index

Notes on the index and on the plates

The descriptions of the objects given in chapter 2 have been grouped together according to category Thus the numbering sequence in the museum's catalogue was not used as a basis for the arrangement of the material. As regards the plates, the aim was to bring together objects belonging to the same group. However for reasons of space it was sometimes necessary to insert some illustrations without regard to context.

An index of the objects, based on the catalogue numbers (which also appear in the illustrations) has been devised in order to make it easier for reader to find where an object is described and where it is discussed in chapters 3–5 By this means crossreferences in the text have also been avoided.

Some English tool names may be difficult for the nonspecialist Scandinavian scholar to understand, in some cases, therefore, the Swedish name has also been included in the index.

Plates

* An asterisk on the plates in place of a number indicates that an object is unnumbered.
( ) A bracket round the number of the plates in the index indicates that only a part (or parts) of the object is illustrated.
   A dash in place of a plate number indicates that the numbered fragment is not illustrated.
Note to pls. 15–30. When the object is illustrated in section it is hatched, whereas a plain outline (e.g. pl. 21) represents a side view
Note to pls. 25 and 30. Pls. 25 and 30 illustrate only some examples of the fragments which are numbered 125 and 126. The fragments not included here are illustrated in the archives of ATA.

The majority of the photographs were taken by Märta Claréus, Nordiska museet. Drawings for pls. 15–30 were executed by Janis Cirulis, now in Newton, Mass. USA. Cover illustration from photograph by Iwar Anderson, Statens Historiska Museum. Some photographs have been provided by ATA (pls. 2:2–3, 10:2–3, 13:2 and 14:1). Bengt Händel, Statens Historiska Museum, replaced Cirulis's lost drawing of the steelyard and is also responsible for the illustration of the detail of the chest's lock, fig. 2, the whetstone no. 122 and of the axe, fig. 5. Maps pls. 31 and 32 drawn by Britta Eriksson and Alicja Grenberger Gustavianum, Uppsala.

Pl. 1

Pl. 2

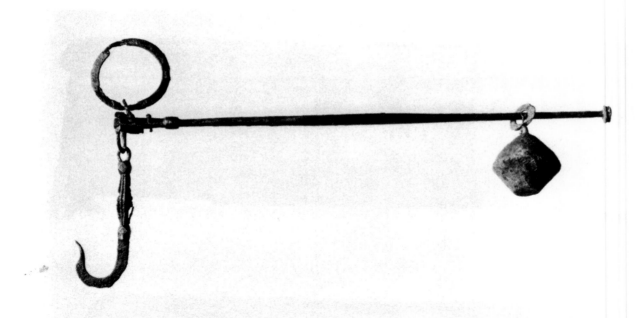

The steelyard no. 1

The steelyard no. 1 details.

Pl. 3

Fire-grid no. 31

Pl. 4

Trace-rings no. 87–90.

The keys no. 2–3.

Pl. 5

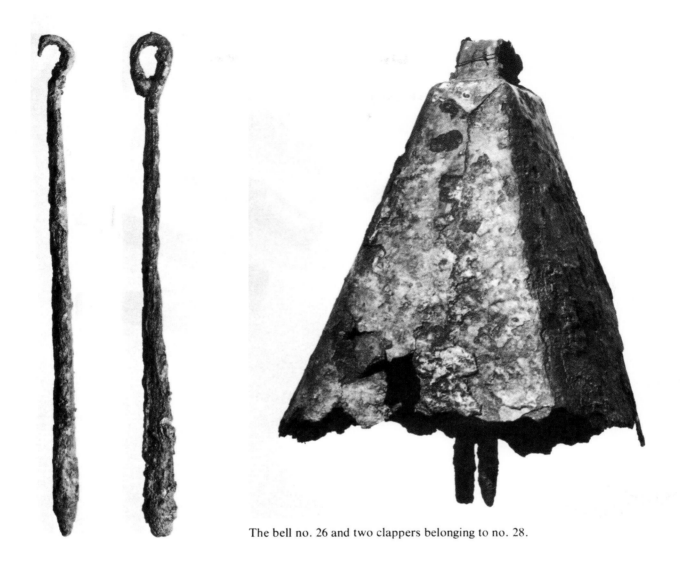

The bell no. 26 and two clappers belonging to no. 28.

The padlocks no. 10–12.

Pl. 6

Sledge hammers no. 69–71 and hammers no. 65–67

The tongs no. 44 with iron bar no. 110, and the plate-shears no. 45, with the griddle no. 18.

Pl. 7

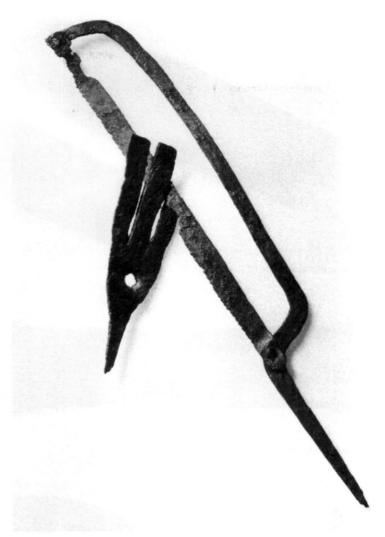

The tongs no. 44.

The hack-saw no. 36; with lockspring no. 7

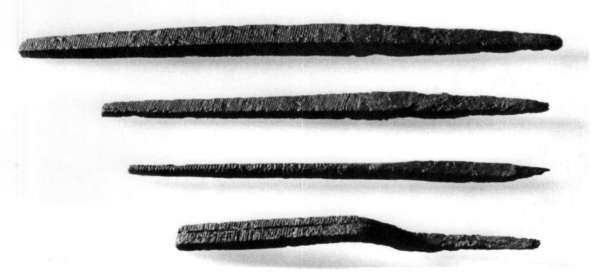

The files no. 32–34, and the rasp no. 38.

Pl. 8

The iron tools no. 104–105.

The hammer no. 68.

The anvil no. 75.

The underlays no. 77–78.

Pl. 9

The tripod stands no. 92–93.

The anvils no. 72–74.

Pl. 10

The cauldron-handels no. 22 and 20.

The stamping pad no 85.   A cauldron fragment **

Pl. 11

The cauldron no. 19.

The cauldron no. 23–24.

Pl. 12

Adzes. no. 63 and 64, axes no 61 and 62. Chisel no. 59.

Axe no. 62.

Nail-making iron no. 86.

Pl. 13

Moulding-iron no. 54, and draw-knife no. 54.

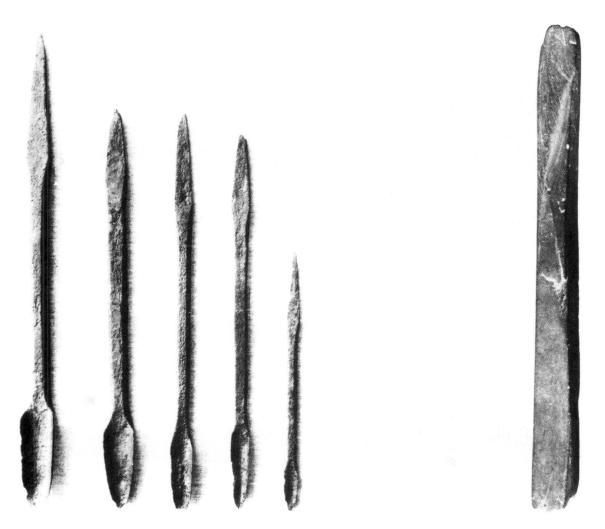

Spoon-angers no. 46–50.

Whetstone no. 123.

Pl. 14

The saw no. 42 and the saw-blade no. 41

The (?) scribing tool no. 97 and the tool no. 96.

The iron bars no. 110-111

Pl. 15

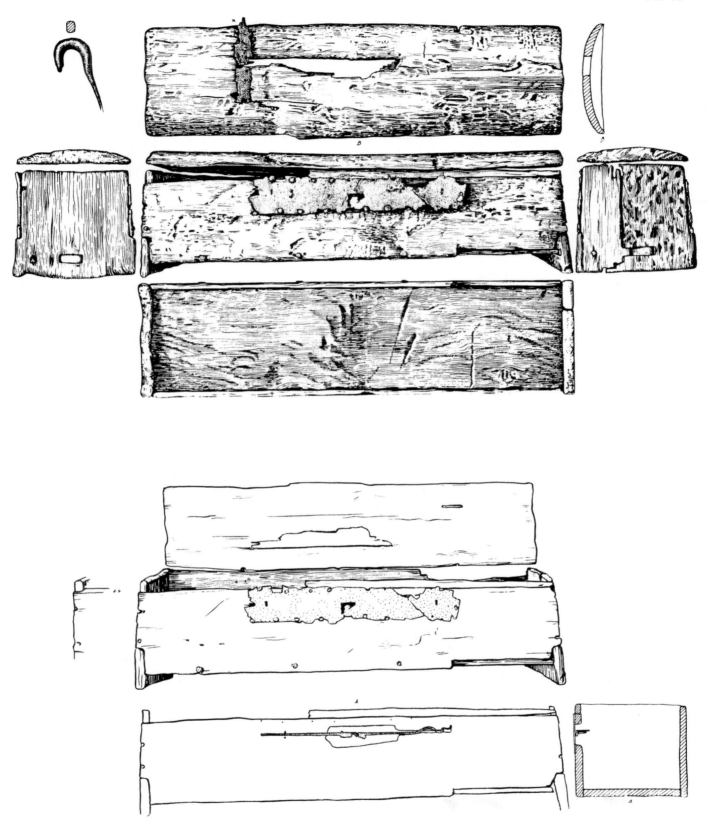

Pl. 15.   Scale 1:8, the hinge detail 1:2.

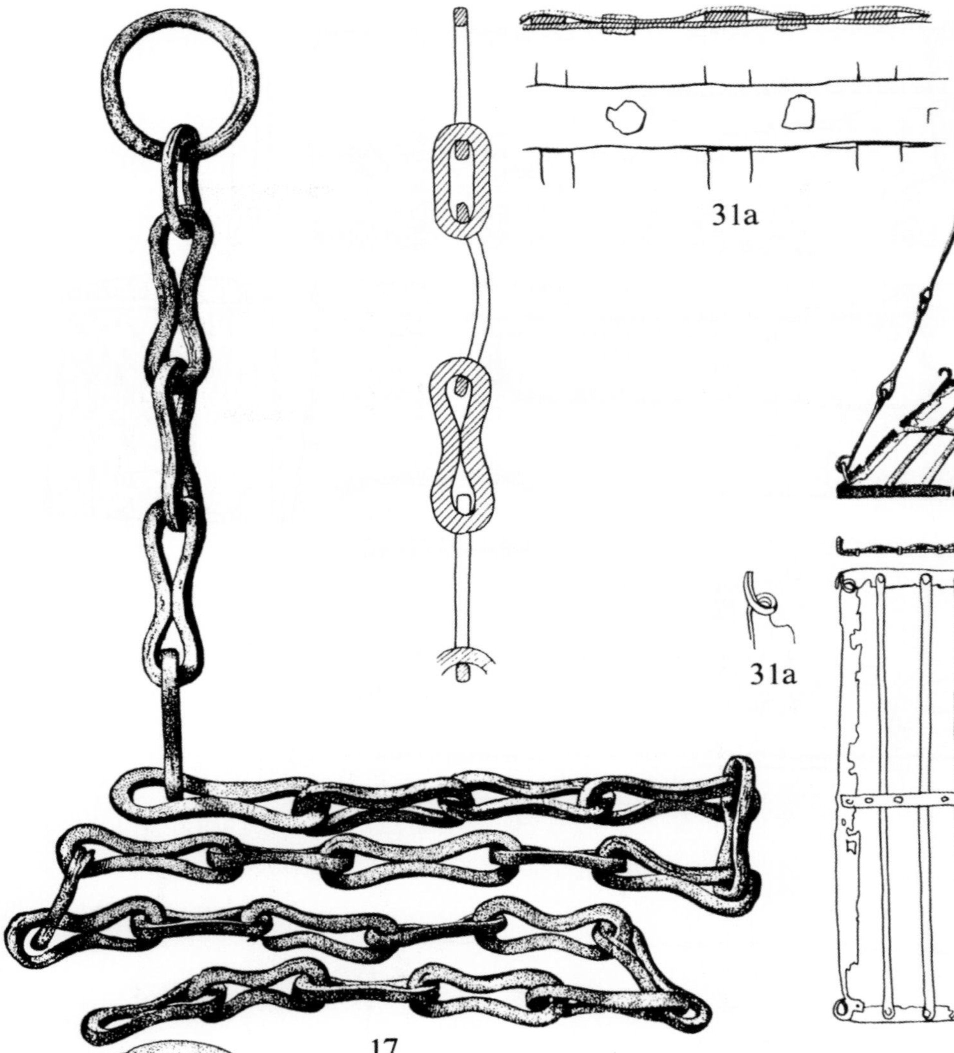

Pl. 16

31a

31a

17

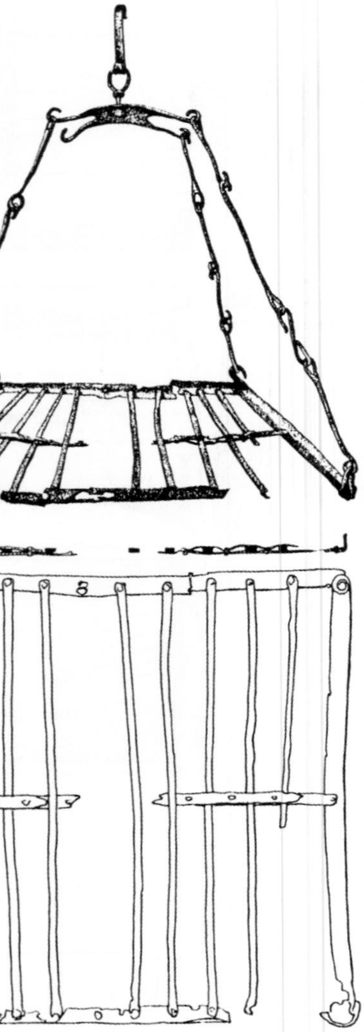

31

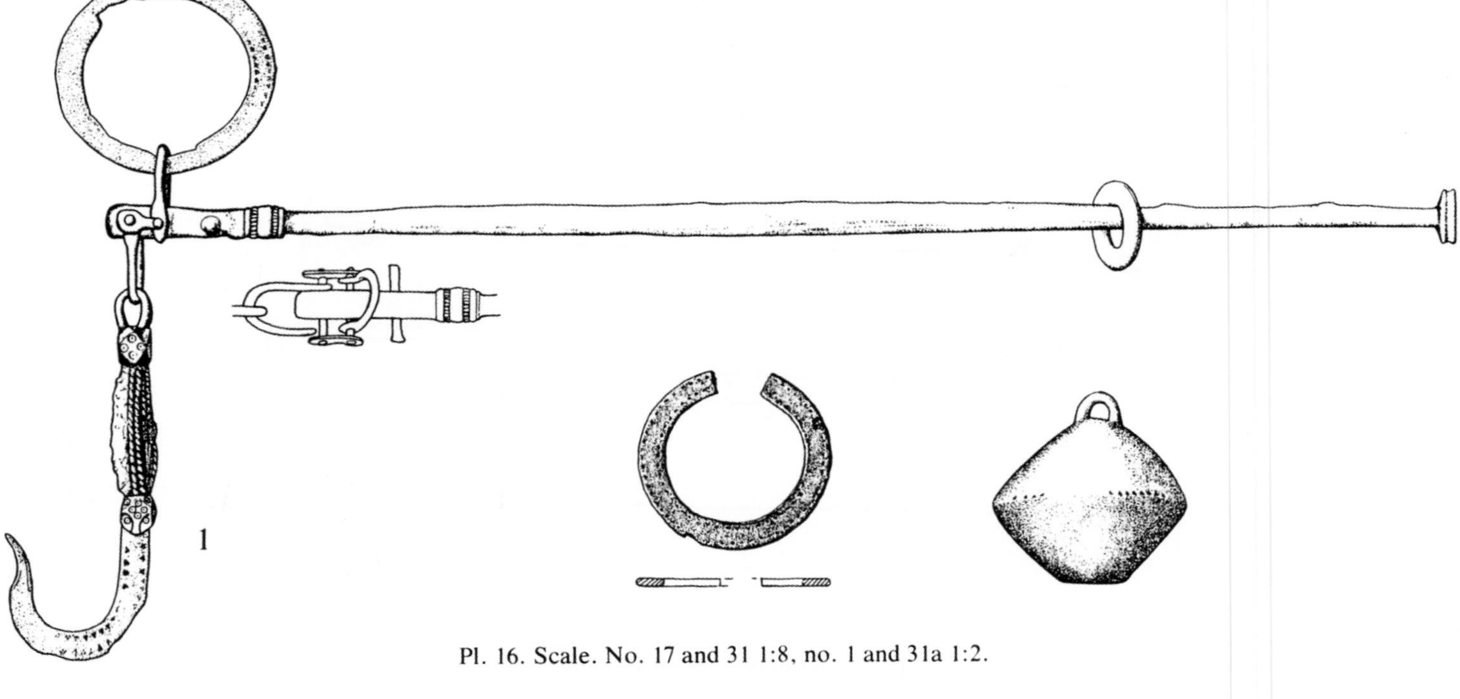

1

Pl. 16. Scale. No. 17 and 31 1:8, no. 1 and 31a 1:2.

Pl. 17

26

27

28

27a

Pl. 17 Scale 1:4 and ca. 1:4.

Pl. 18

87

88

89

91

90

Pl. 18. Scale 1:2.

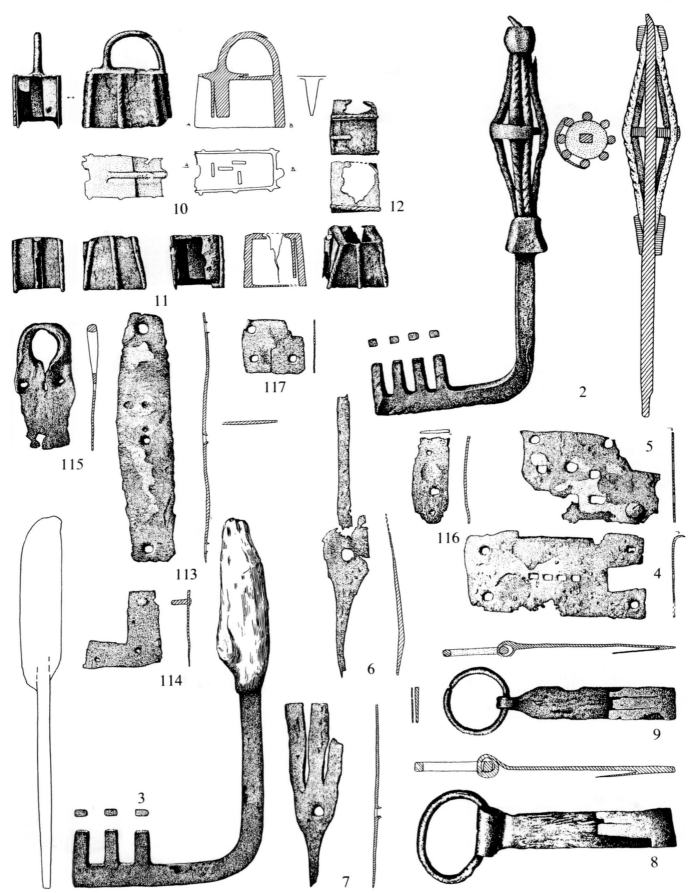

Pl. 19

10

12

11

117

2

5

115

113

116

4

114

3

6

7

9

8

Pl. 19. Scale 1:2.

Pl. 20

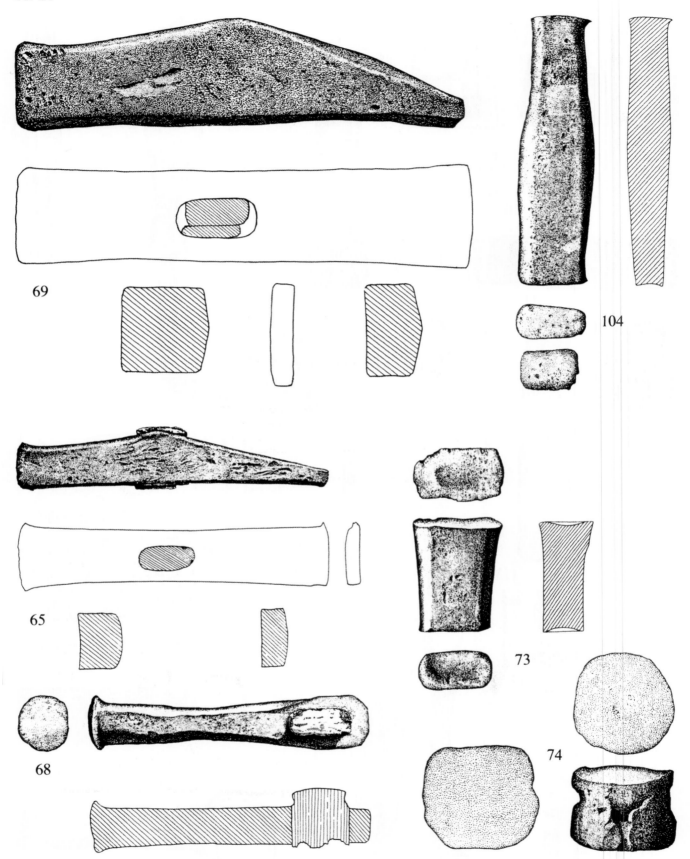

69

104

65

73

68

74

Pl. 20. Scale 1:2.

Pl. 21

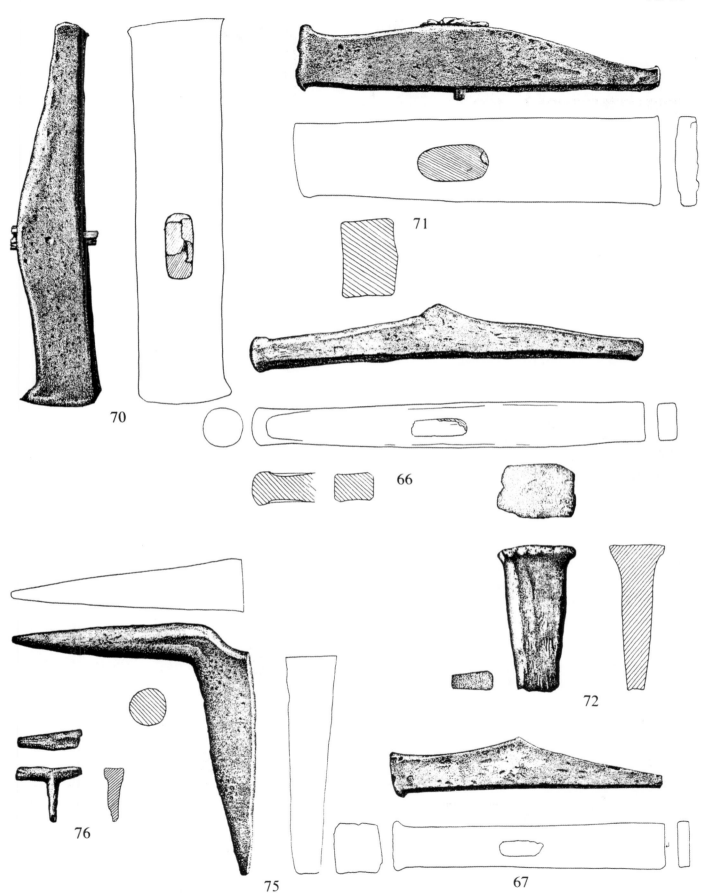

70

71

66

72

76

75

67

Pl. 21 Scale 1:2.

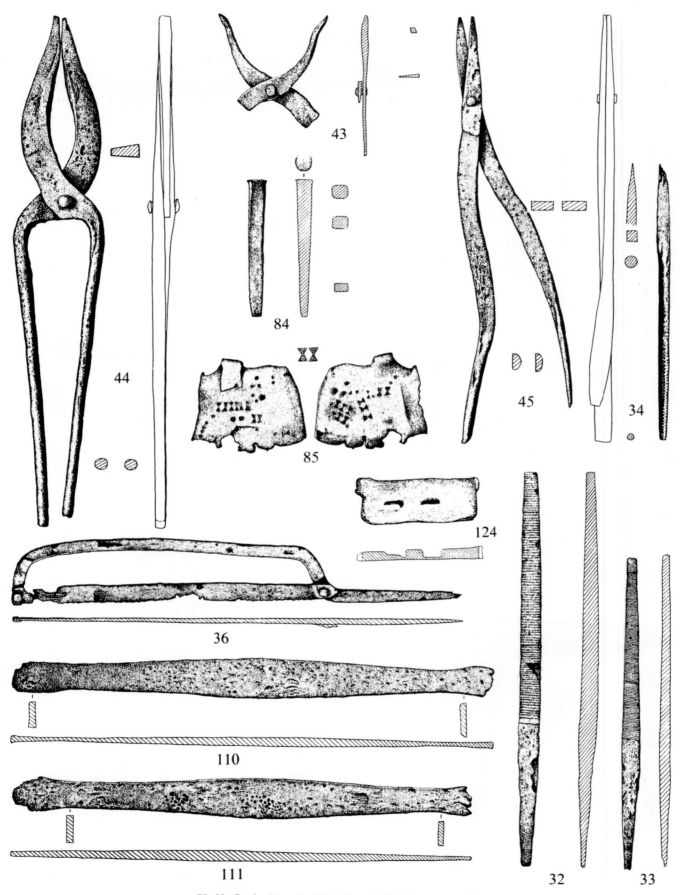

Pl. 22

44

43

84

85

45

34

124

36

110

111

32

33

Pl. 22. Scale. No. 44, 45, 110 and 111 1:4, the rest 1:2.

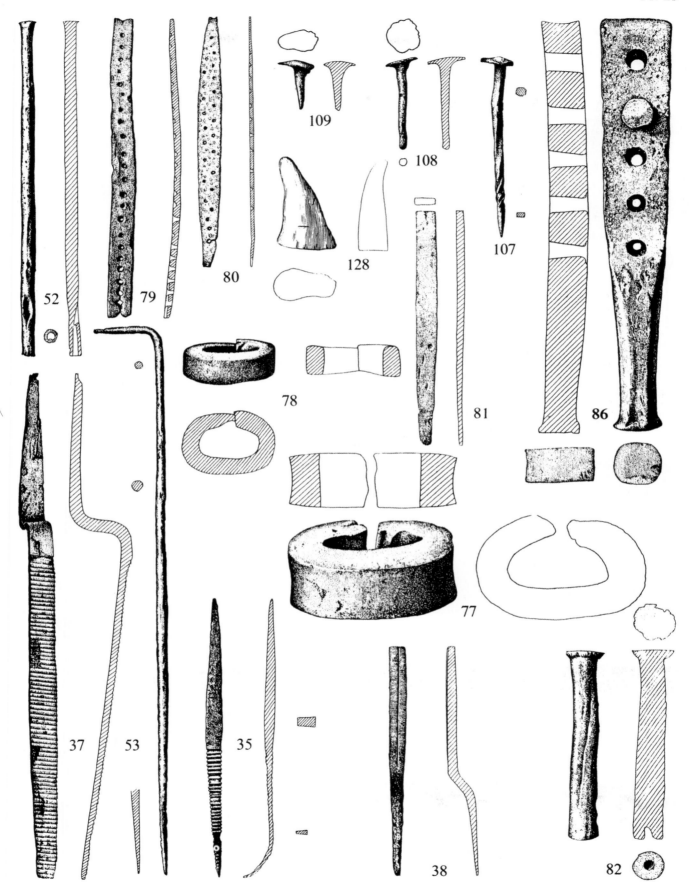

Pl. 23. Scale No. 52 1:4, the rest 1:2.

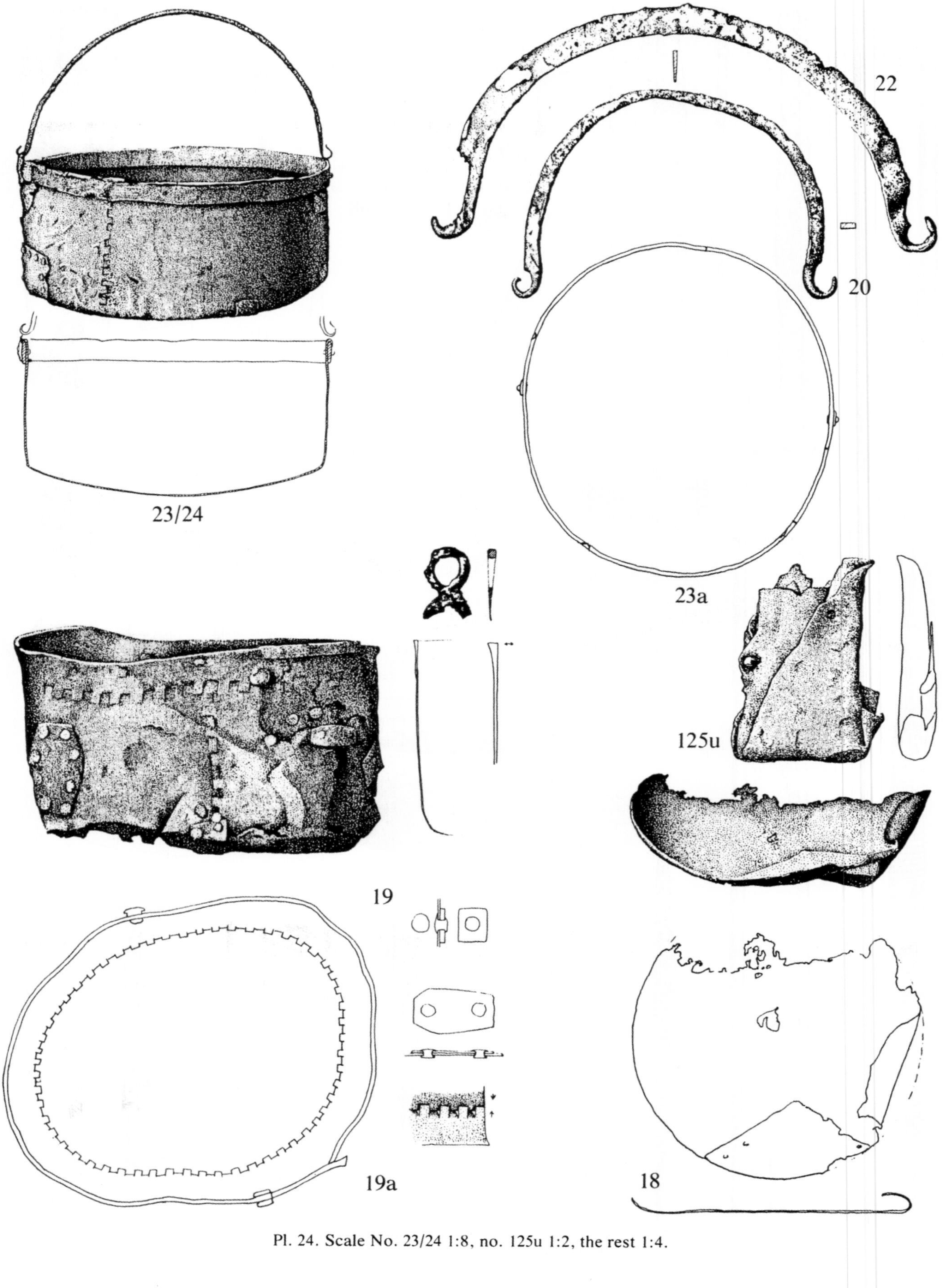

Pl. 24

23/24

22

20

23a

125u

19

19a

18

Pl. 24. Scale No. 23/24 1:8, no. 125u 1:2, the rest 1:4.

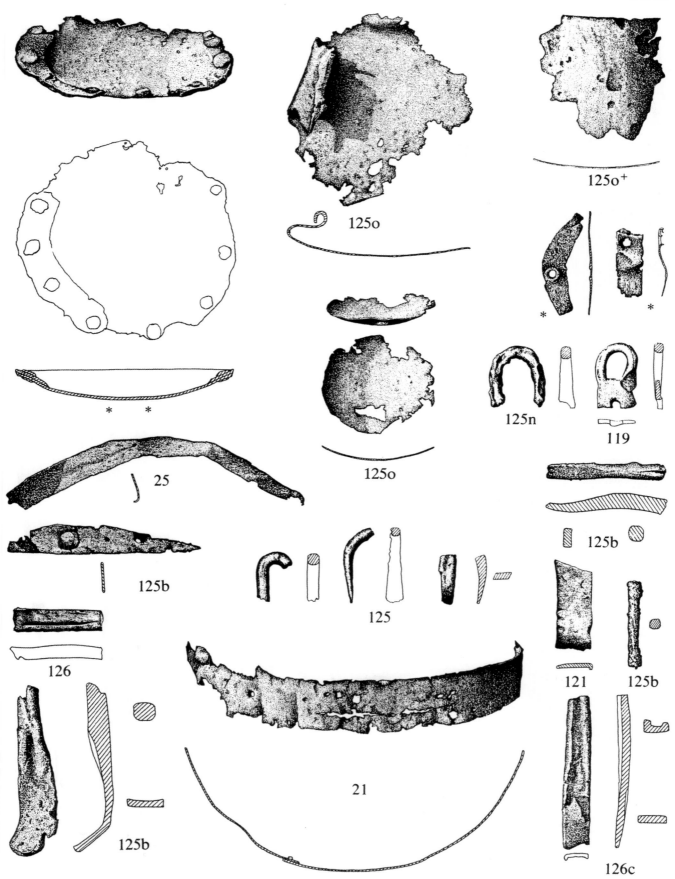

125o⁺

125o

125o

125n   119

25

125b

125b

125

125b

126

121   125b

21

126c

125b

Pl. 25. Scale. No. 21 1:6, no. 125o⁺ 1:4, the rest 1:2.

Pl. 26

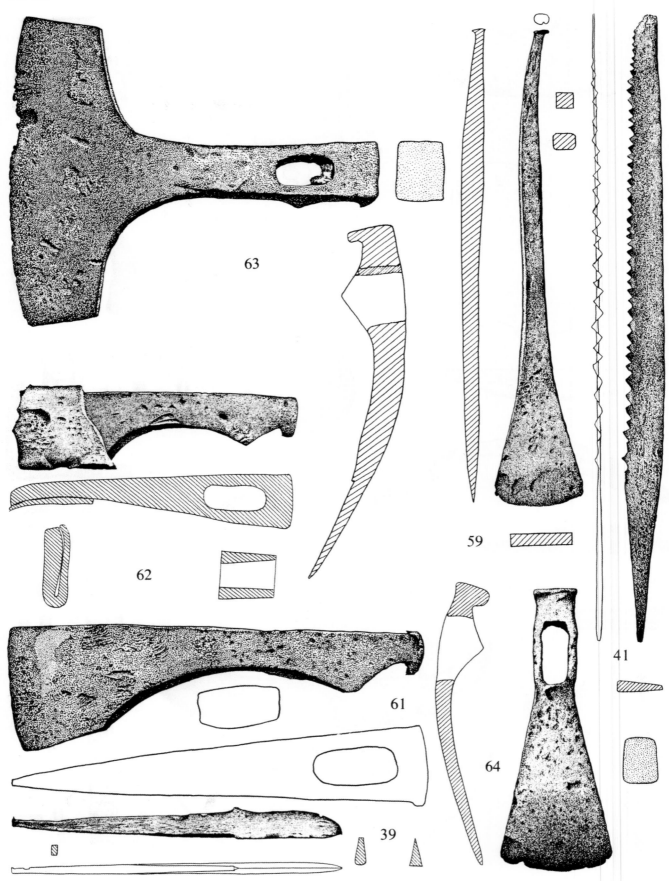

Pl. 26. Scale 1:2.

Pl. 27

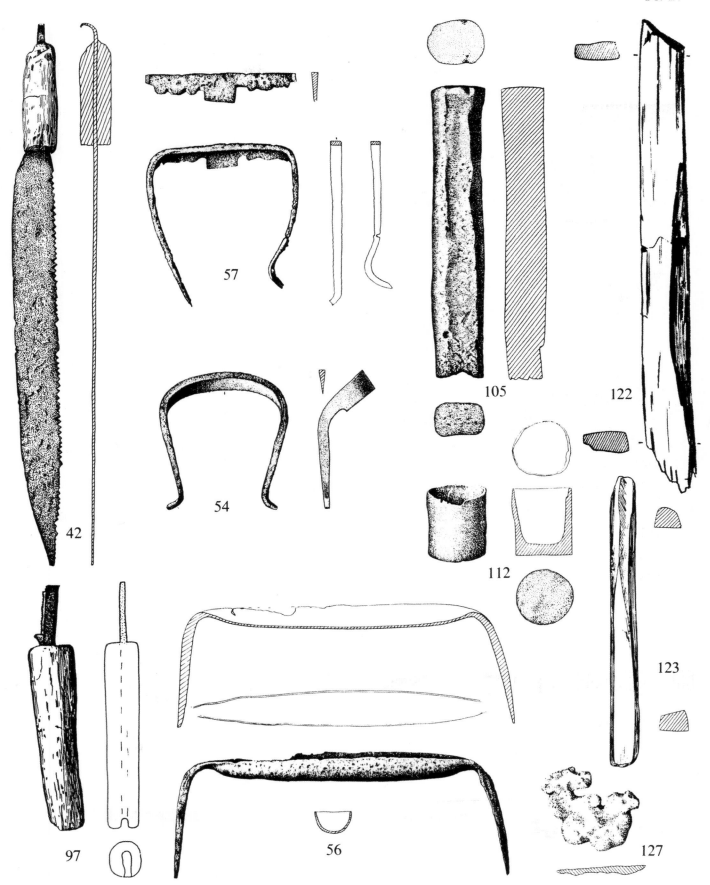

42

57

54

97

56

105

112

122

123

127

Pl. 27 Scale. No. 42 1:4, no. 122 ca. 1:3, the rest 1:2.

Pl. 28

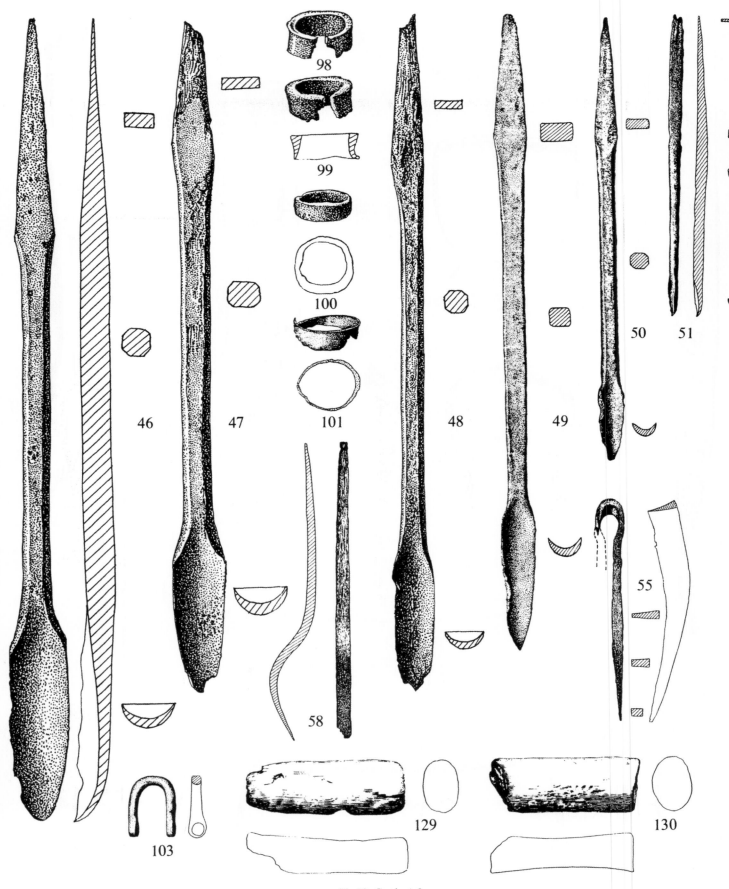

98

99

100

101

46   47   58   48   49   50   51

103   129   130   55

Pl. 28. Scale 1:2.

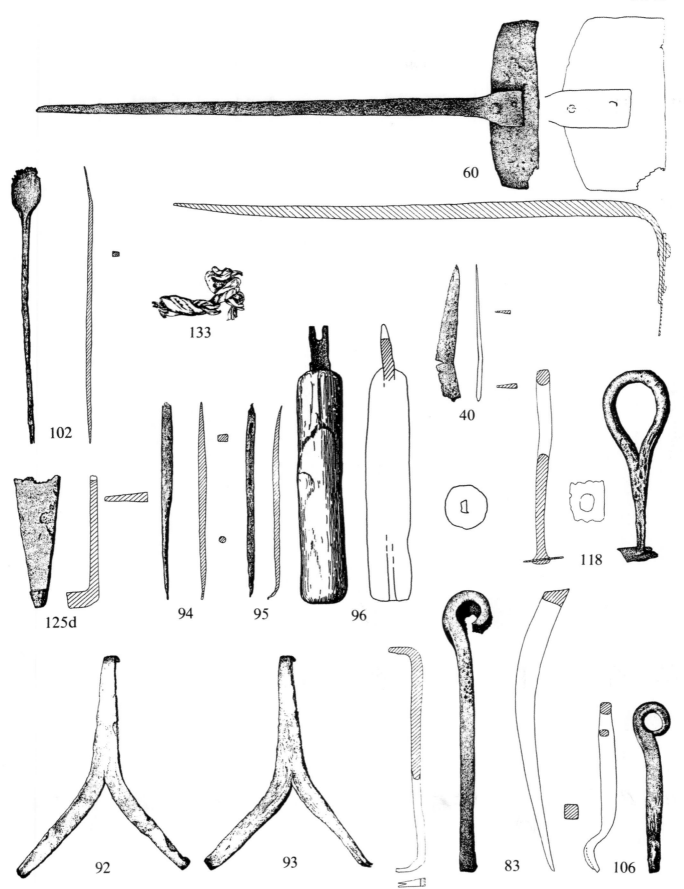

Pl. 29

Pl. 29. Scale 1:2.

Pl. 30

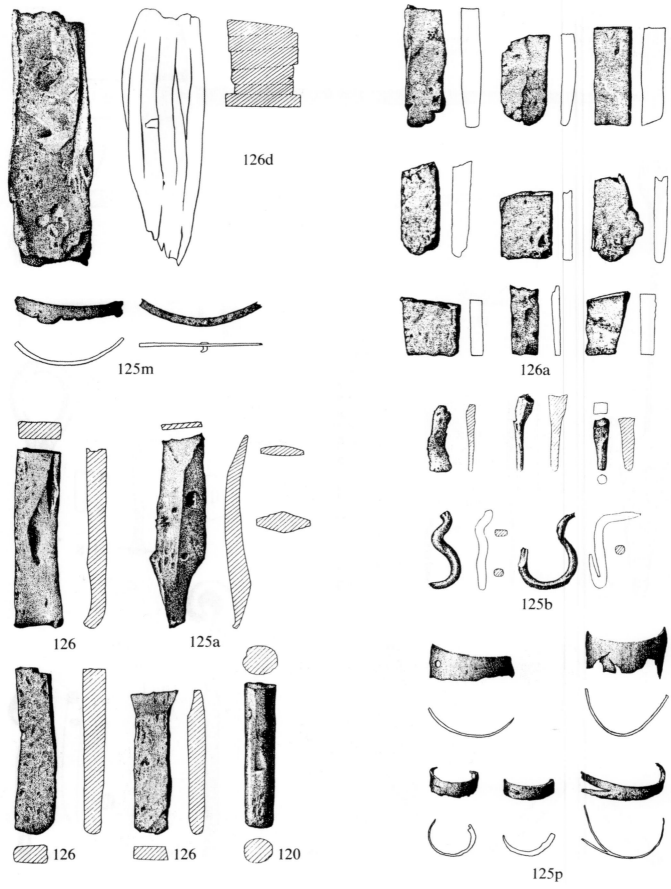

126d

125m

126

125a

126a

125b

126 126 120

125p

Pl. 30. Scale 1:2.

Pl. 31

Pl. 31.1. The Mästermyr region from a survey map (ATA). 1) parish boundary 2) major road, 3) minor road, 4) channel, S) common land (gravel pit). ● marks the presumed find spot.

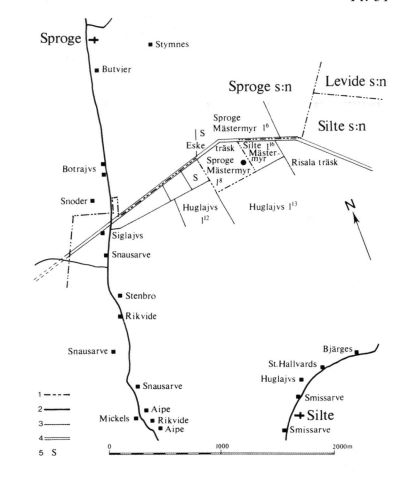

Pl. 31:2 Detailed map of Mästermyr based on surveys in 1903–1908. After Ljungqvist 1914, pl. 2. Some places names have been added, and some details of the vegetation distribution excluded. Key to map: 1) Fen land boundary· 2) Marginal lagg; 3) Moraine ridges in swamps; 4) Woods; 5) Direction of flow i.e. streams; 6) Drainage channel. *Note:* The Swedish terms are explained in more detail in Appendix I.

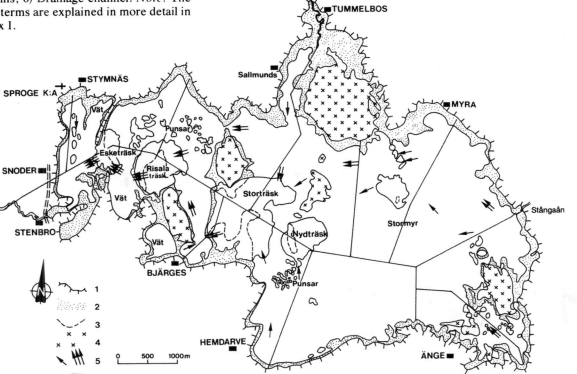

Pl. 32

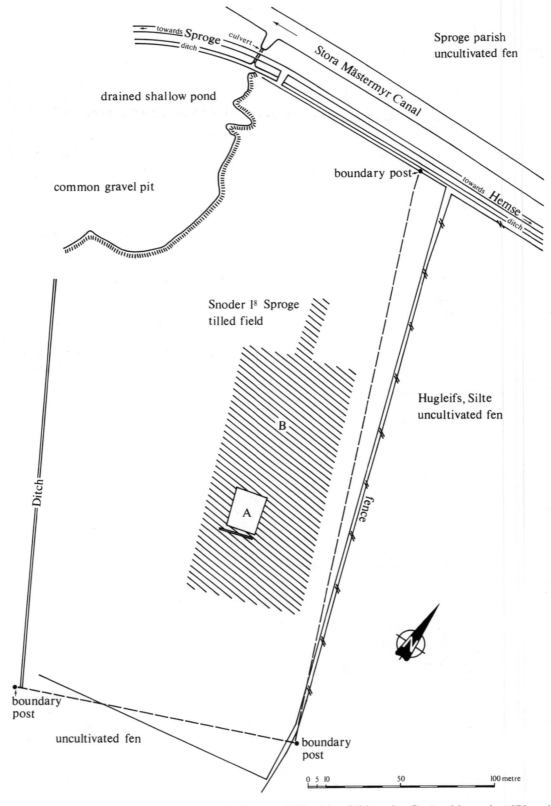

towards Sproge

culvert

ditch

Stora Mästermyr Canal

Sproge parish
uncultivated fen

drained shallow pond

boundary post

towards Hemse

ditch

common gravel pit

Snoder 1⁸ Sproge
tilled field

Hugleifs, Silte
uncultivated fen

B

Ditch

A

fence

N

boundary
post

uncultivated fen

boundary
post

0 5 10   50   100 metre

Pl. 32. Map of the find area at Mästermyr by M. Stenberger 1937 with additions by G. Arwidsson in 1979 and 1981. A = excavations in 1937· B = investigated area in 1979 and 1981